William S. Burroughs

Twayne's United States Authors Series

Warren French, Editor

Indiana University, Indianapolis

WILLIAM S. BURROUGHS in New York City
Photograph courtesy of Gerard Malanga

William S. Burroughs

By Jennie Skerl

Twayne Publishers • *Boston*

William S. Burroughs

Jennie Skerl

Copyright © 1985 by G. K. Hall & Company
All Rights Reserved
Published by Twayne Publishers
A Division of G. K. Hall & Company
70 Lincoln Street
Boston, Massachusetts 02111

First Paperback Edition, 1986

Book production by Elizabeth Todesco
Book design by Barbara Anderson

Printed on permanent/durable acid-free
paper and bound in the United States of
America

Library of Congress Cataloging in Publication Data

Skerl, Jennie.
    William S. Burroughs.

    (Twayne's United States authors series; TUSAS 438)
    Bibliography: p. 111.
    Includes index.
    1. Burroughs, William S., 1914–
—Criticism and interpretation.
I. Title.   II. Series.
PS3552.U75Z85   1985   813'.54   84-27899
ISBN 0-8057-7438-6
ISBN 0-8057-7456-4 (pbk.)

Contents

About the Author

Jennie Skerl has a B.A., M.A., and Ph.D. in English with a specialization in modern literature. She has been on the faculties of Utica College of Syracuse University, Rensselaer Polytechnic Institute, and Skidmore College and is currently a Visiting Faculty Fellow at Skidmore and the recipient of an NEH Research Fellowship for 1984–85. She has published essays on William S. Burroughs, Samuel Beckett, James Joyce, literary theory, and the teaching of writing. Her primary research interests are avant-garde fiction and narrative theory.

Preface

I have written this book out of admiration for William S. Burroughs the artist. An innovator whose current reputation is largely based on one book, *Naked Lunch*, Burroughs has not yet received the careful critical attention due an achievement that goes beyond this seminal work. Readers who wish to read about Burroughs must search through periodical indexes for journal articles and must find the several critical books that discuss Burroughs only in developing a larger literary thesis. Eric Mottram's *William Burroughs: The Algebra of Need* (1977) stands alone as an overview of Burroughs's work, but this insightful study, an example of postmodern criticism, extends the experimentalism of Burroughs's art to the critical realm. There is no standard critical introduction to Burroughs's work aimed at the general reader and the community of literary historians. This volume aims to fill that need and to promote a greater appreciation of Burroughs's artistry.

Chapter 1, which outlines Burroughs's biography, depends upon the research of others, but also attempts to correct many previously published errors. Much is known about the Burroughs legend and little about the man himself. The creation of legend is a part of Burroughs's art that must be separated from fact by the literary historian but incorporated into his oeuvre by the literary critic. I have attempted this difficult task and have no doubt succeeded only partially. I hope, at least, that I have adequately defined the problem of the Burroughs legend as a *literary* problem.

In chapter 1, I also put forth the thesis that hipsterism as a worldview is the source of Burroughs's art. This thesis informs the chronological discussion of Burroughs's works that follows in chapters 2, 3, and 4. I confine my detailed analysis to Burroughs's novels and discuss other works only when they shed light upon themes and techniques in the novels. The reader of this volume will quickly realize that this conventional approach to Burroughs's fiction to some extent falsifies the nature of his work. For Burroughs is not strictly a novelist, and his fictions cannot be conveniently classified into major and minor works. In fact, it is the purpose of his art to destroy such categories. However, Burroughs's own decision to publish novels through major publishing houses does lend authority to this approach, and chronological analysis does emphasize Burroughs's evolution as an artist, which *is* important to his theory and practice. Furthermore, studying Burroughs's development as a writer also makes the "one book" that is Burroughs's fiction more comprehensible to those who are not already familiar with the body of his work.

Interpreting the work of a living writer is an open-ended process with no definite conclusion. I have chosen to end my survey of Burroughs's fiction with the 1981 publication of *Cities of the Red Night,* a novel that is a culmination of recent themes, if not the end of a series. The bibliography lists works and criticism up to 1982. Needless to say, my final assessment is a tentative one, but one that makes a strong case for Burroughs's contribution to literature. I hope I have shown that Burroughs can be accurately judged only when placed in the avant-garde context in which he belongs.

Within the text, the following abbreviations are used in references to Burroughs's works: E (*Exterminator!*); J (*Junkie*); NE (*Nova Express*); NL (*Naked Lunch*); TTE (*The Ticket That Exploded*); WB (*The Wild Boys*); YL (*The Yage Letters*).

I wish to thank the many friends, colleagues, and students who, knowingly or not, have contributed to this book. I must especially thank my husband, John L. Hynes, for his constant encouragement and editorial advice. I am grateful to William S. Burroughs for granting me an interview and for permission to quote from his works. I also thank James Grauerholz, Mr. Burroughs's secretary, for his help and encouragement. Thanks to David A. Roberts and Randy Crick for reading the manuscript at a crucial stage, and to Robin Lydenberg for reviewing the final bibliography. Grants from Utica College of Syracuse University and from Skidmore College helped me, respectively, to begin and to conclude this project.

Jennie Skerl

Skidmore College

Chronology

1914   William Seward Burroughs born on 5 February 1914 in St. Louis, Missouri, the second son of Mortimer P. and Laura Lee Burroughs.

1920–1932   Attends the John Burroughs School and the Taylor School in the St. Louis area. Attends the Los Alamos Ranch School in New Mexico.

1932–1936   Attends Harvard University, majors in English, receives bachelor's degree.

1936–1937   Attends medical school at the University of Vienna, travels in Europe, marries Ilse Herzfeld Klapper.

1938   Attends graduate school in anthropology at Harvard, lives with Kells Elvins, with whom he writes "Twilight's Last Gleamings" (later included in *Nova Express*).

1942   Briefly serves in the United States Army.

1944   After settling in New York (in 1943), meets Jack Kerouac, Allen Ginsberg, Joan Vollmer Adams, Edie Parker, and others of their circle. Introduced to morphine by Herbert Huncke and becomes an addict.

1945   Collaborates with Kerouac on a novel, "And the Hippos Were Boiled in Their Tanks" (unpublished).

1946   Divorces Ilse Burroughs, thereafter lives with Joan Vollmer as his common-law wife. Leaves New York with Joan Burroughs and her infant daughter, settles near New Waverly, Texas.

1947   William Burroughs, Jr., born on 21 July 1947 in Conroe, Texas.

1948   Admits himself to the United States Public Health Service Hospital in Lexington, Kentucky, to treat his addiction. Moves with his family to Algiers, Louisiana, across the river from New Orleans.

1949   Arrested for possession of illegal drugs and firearms, flees to Mexico City with his family.

1950   Begins writing *Junkie,* mails chapters to Ginsberg.

1951   Accidentally shoots and kills Joan Burroughs on 6 September 1951. Their children are sent to live with their grandparents.

1952   *Junkie* is accepted for publication with the help of Ginsberg and Carl Solomon. Begins writing "Queer" (unpublished). After his legal case is settled in Mexico, he travels to Central America and Tangier.

1953   Travels in South America for several months, sending letters to Ginsberg. During brief residence in New York in the fall, Burroughs and Ginsberg edit letters to create "In Search of Yage." Returns to Tangier in December and settles there; begins writing *Naked Lunch. Junkie* published by Ace Books as a doubledecker paperback with *Narcotic Agent* by Maurice Helbrant.

1957   Travels to London to treat his addiction. Ginsberg and Kerouac visit Burroughs in Tangier and help with the *Naked Lunch* manuscript. Paul Bowles introduces Burroughs to Brion Gysin, an important friend and collaborator. "Letter from a Master Addict to Dangerous Drugs" published in the *British Journal of Addiction.* Part of *Naked Lunch* is published in the *Black Mountain Review.*

1958–1965   Resides in Paris, London, and Tangier.

1958   Gysin and Sinclair Beiles help to prepare *Naked Lunch* for publication.

1959   *The Naked Lunch* published in Paris. Begins to edit the trilogy: *The Soft Machine, The Ticket That Exploded, Nova Express.* Portions of *Naked Lunch* and "In Quest of Yage" published in *Big Table*; the first issue of this journal is seized by the Post Office. Introduced to the cutup by Gysin.

1960   Publishes first cutup experiments in *The Exterminator* in the United States and *Minutes To Go* in Paris. "Deposition: Testimony Concerning a Sickness" published in *Evergreen Review.*

1961   *The Soft Machine* published in Paris. "Roosevelt After Inauguration" published in *Floating Bear* and seized by the Post Office. "From *Naked Lunch*" published in *Evergreen Review.*

1962   *Naked Lunch* published in the United States by Grove Press. The publisher prepares for a legal battle. *The Ticket That Exploded* published in Paris.

1962–1964   *Naked Lunch* is widely reviewed in the United States and England and stirs a major literary controversy.

1963   Legal proceedings begin against *Naked Lunch* in Boston. *Dead Fingers Talk* published in London. *The Yage Letters* published in the United States.

1964   *Nova Express* published in the United States.

1965   Resides in the United States, primarily New York. Burroughs's father dies. Boston trial of *Naked Lunch* begins. The book is declared to be obscene and the case is appealed. The case against *Naked Lunch* is dropped in Los Angeles. Burroughs creates several experimental films with Antony Balch and Brion Gysin.

1966–1974   Resides in London.

1966   The Massachusetts Supreme Court rules that *Naked Lunch* is not obscene and lifts the ban on sales. *The Soft Machine* published in the United States.

1967   *The Ticket That Exploded* published in the United States.

1968   Attends the Democratic National Convention in Chicago for *Esquire,* which published "Coming of the Purple Better One."

1969   Jack Kerouac dies.

1970   Burroughs's mother dies. *The Job* published in the States. *The Last Words of Dutch Schultz* published in London.

1971   *The Wild Boys* published in the United States.

1973   *Exterminator!* published in the United States.

1974   Moves to New York, teaches for one semester at City College of New York, begins spending summers in residence at the Jack Kerouac School of Disembodied Poetics at Naropa Institute in Boulder, Colorado.

1975   *Port of Saints* published in London. *The Last Words of Dutch Schultz, The Book of Breeething* published in the United States.

1976   *Cobble Stone Gardens* and *The Retreat Diaries* published in the United States.

1977   *Junky,* the complete and unexpurgated text (with revised spelling of title), published in the United States.

1978   The Nova Convention in honor of William S. Burroughs held in New York. *The Third Mind* published in the United States.

1979   *Blade Runner* and *Roosevelt After Inauguration* published in the United States.

1980   *Port of Saints* published in the United States.

1981   Death of William Burroughs, Jr. *Cities of the Red Night* published in the United States.

1982   *Letters to Allen Ginsberg* published in the United States.

1983   Burroughs's brother, Mortimer, dies. Burroughs is inducted into the American Academy and Institute of Arts and Letters.

Chapter One
The Hipster as Artist

William S. Burroughs's career as writer and oracle of the Beat Generation is legendary. His biography is known to the public largely through the homage of his friends Jack Kerouac and Allen Ginsberg and through his own semiautobiographical novels. Perhaps the best known portrait of Burroughs is Jack Kerouac's description of him as "Old Bull Lee" in *On the Road*. He describes Burroughs as an eccentric scholar and traveler, a seeker of "the facts of life," who fascinated his friends with his stories and theories:

He spent all his time talking and teaching others. Jane sat at his feet; so did I; so did Dean; and so had Carlo Marx. We'd all learned from him. He was a gray, nondescript-looking fellow you wouldn't notice on the street, unless you looked closer and saw his mad, bony skull with its strange youthfulness—a Kansas minister with exotic, phenomenal fires and mysteries. He had studied medicine in Vienna; had studied anthropology, read everything; and now he was settling to his life's work, which was the study of things themselves in the streets of life and the night.[1]

Although the chapter about Bull Lee on his farm outside New Orleans is not an inaccurate description of Burroughs, it is a portrayal subtly transformed by Kerouac's mythopoeic imagination.

Burroughs's self-portrait in his own semiautobiographical novels also contributes to the creation of a legend. Although he uses his own experience as the basis for his fiction, he shapes and organizes it to fit an artistic pattern: the writer who has spent a season in hell and returned to tell his story. He often portrays himself as a character, but one devoid of introspection and, therefore, without an inner life. Thus Burroughs is able to objectify himself in his work in such a way as to depersonalize the biographical material and give it mythic power.

Yet the part of himself that Burroughs omits from his works, the time-bound personality's intimate feelings and relationships, is the self the biographer seeks to record. A detailed factual narrative of Burroughs's life is the job of future researchers. This chapter is an interpretive account that attempts to remain close to the known facts, but which necessarily follows the outline of a myth. For in spite of his disclaimers, Burroughs seems consciously to have chosen to pattern his life on the postromantic artist's quest in the tradition of the *poète maudit*. Like many others of that tradition, Burroughs makes it difficult to draw the line between life and art, and his most important "work" may be his legend, which exists somewhere between the realms of fact and fiction, partaking of both.

Youth: Privilege and Alienation

William Seward Burroughs was born on 5 February 1914 in St. Louis, Missouri, into a prominent family. Burroughs's father, Mortimer P. Burroughs, was the son of the man who invented the adding machine and founded the company that bears his name. Burroughs is his paternal grandfather's namesake. Burroughs's mother, Laura Lee Burroughs, was the daughter of a distinguished minister whose family claimed descent from Robert E. Lee. In the marriage of Burroughs's parents the northern and southern strains of the American Protestant tradition and its ruling elite were united. Burroughs's paternal grandfather, originally from Auburn, New York, was an example of Yankee ingenuity and commercial success; and his maternal grandfather, James Wideman Lee, a Methodist Episcopal minister in Atlanta and St. Louis, eloquently preached the Calvinist doctrine that inspired men like William S. Burroughs I. Their grandson inherited both the inventiveness of the one and the verbal skill of the other, and both talents are evident in his work.

The Lee family background, in particular, may have influenced some of Burroughs's major preoccupations as a writer. Reverend James W. Lee and his son, Ivy Ledbetter Lee, were both talented speakers and writers who used their abilities to justify the social order. Reverend Lee was the author of several religious books and a persuasive speaker. A liberal southerner for his time and a master at conciliation, Lee tried to accommodate new ideas and social forces into the established church. He was very popular and successful as a Methodist Episcopal pastor, ending his career as Presiding Elder of St. Louis.[2] Ivy Lee, Burroughs's uncle, used the family talent with words and personal relations to serve the great capitalists of his time as the first public-relations man. He made advertising and public relations the Lee family business, bringing his two sons into his firm.

Ivy Lee first achieved fame and success as the public-relations man for the Rockefellers during the Ludlow Massacre in 1914. He went on to serve many industrialists and corporations, guiding them through a turbulent period of muckraking and reform. Like his father, Ivy Lee was a conciliator who taught his clients to acknowledge public opinion and accommodate social change in order to preserve their power. Lee thought the best response to the muckrakers was to make use of the same media and their persuasive techniques to present business in a positive light. Furthermore, he believed that the way to persuade the masses was through "symbols and phrases," not reason and facts.[3] Lee was often attacked by radicals and reformers who denounced him as a sinister manipulator. Upton Sinclair gave him the nickname of "Poison Ivy,"[4] and he was the basis for J. Ward Moorehouse in Dos Passos's *U.S.A.* trilogy.[5] He died under attack in 1934, shortly after appearing before the Congressional Committee on Un-American Activities to explain his work for the I.G. Farben Company under the Nazi regime.[6]

Since Ivy Lee was the most famous and successful member of the Lee family, Burroughs could hardly have been unaware of Ivy's career and the moral questions it posed, especially since Ivy's success exactly spans the years of Burroughs's youth from 1914, the year of his birth, to 1934, when he was a college student. As a writer Burroughs carries on the Lee tradition of eloquence, of swaying men with "symbols and phrases," but he uses his talent to attack men like James and Ivy Lee and the social order they protected. Indeed, in his experimental trilogy—*The Soft Machine, The Ticket That Exploded,* and *Nova Express*—Burroughs's main purpose is to attack the manipulation of the common man through words and images, and the experimental prose is an attempt to counteract that control through Burroughs's own "word-and-image" techniques. Burroughs seems to acknowledge and, at the same time, ironically reject the Lee heritage in his use of the family name as a pseudonym in his novels. Burroughs first published *Junkie* under the name "William Lee," and in his next four novels the character who is his alter ego in fighting the evil forces of control is called Inspector or Agent Lee. In the *Paris Review* interview in 1965, conducted soon after he completed the trilogy, Burroughs mentioned his grandfather and Ivy Lee, the "master image-maker."[7] Then, in partial explanation of his recent fiction, Burroughs compared his prose technique to advertising: "Like the advertising people we talked about, I'm concerned with the precise manipulation of word and image to create an action, not to go out and buy a Coca-Cola, but to create an alteration in the reader's consciousness."[8] Thus Burroughs's denunciation of the social order has a personal basis: it is the rebellion of a disaffected insider.

Little is known about Burroughs's parents or his childhood. In an interview with the author, Burroughs described his parents as quiet, conventional people who were neither very wealthy nor socially active. His father had no connection with the Burroughs company, and in their later years his parents ran a gift and arts shop called Cobble Stone Gardens, first in St. Louis and then in Palm Beach, Florida. For a number of years, they were able to send Burroughs an allowance from their income.[9]

Burroughs is reticent about his family. He describes his parents briefly in *With William Burroughs* by Victor Bockris, but this account is highly selective and obviously fictionalized.[10] His mother is described as enigmatic, complex, intuitive, charming, and abhorrent of bodily functions; and she receives more emphasis than his father, who is hardly described at all. His older brother, Mortimer, Jr., is mentioned briefly. In 1976 Burroughs published *Cobble Stone Gardens,*[11] a short work of fiction dedicated to his parents and containing a few brief, poignant images of them. The book includes photographs of his parents and brother. This work indicates Burroughs's affection for his parents, but tells us nothing factual about them.

After the death of Burroughs's wife in 1951, his parents took in and brought up his son, who later wrote about his father and grandparents in an article in *Esquire* in 1971 and in his book *Kentucky Ham* (1973). William Burroughs, Jr., described his grandparents as follows: "My grandmother was Laura Lee Burroughs, aristocratic, proud, possessed of great strength and a great disgust for all things pertaining to bodily functions. Perhaps one of the most consequential of all the Burroughs family, she had once been extraordinarily beautiful. Mortimer P. Burroughs, her husband, . . . was kind and gentle and, while under Laura's thumb, still provided most of the merriment in the house."[12] He also described his grandmother's final confinement in a nursing home and her death. Thus again, in her grandson's memoir, Laura Lee Burroughs appears to be a stronger personality than her husband.

The strain of misogyny in Burroughs's work and in interviews in the late 1960s and early 1970s, which he himself attributes to his experience with the "Southern matriarchal and racist" society,[13] has led critics such as John Tytell to speculate about Laura Lee Burroughs's character as a source of Burroughs's rebellion.[14] It should be pointed out, however, that Burroughs has never attacked her personally and that his attacks upon women in general are attacks upon women's roles within a certain social structure, of which southern racist society is a chief example. Again, it may be the values represented by the Lee family that had a strong negative influence upon the young Burroughs, rather than the character of his mother. There is no doubt that she herself was a powerful personality and that she must have influenced her son in important ways. But at the present time, it is impossible to discuss the subject with any authority.

Burroughs spent his youth in the St. Louis area and attended private schools in St. Louis and Los Alamos, New Mexico. Limited factual information about his childhood can be found in his fiction (mainly *Junkie, The Wild Boys,* and *Exterminator!*) and in the brief "Literary Autobiography" published in *A Descriptive Catalogue of the William S. Burroughs Archive.*[15] From these sources a portrait of Burroughs's childhood can be pieced together; however, the biography that emerges should be viewed critically as a story shaped by the artist to fit the pattern of legend. In spite of his privileged upbringing, Burroughs portrays only extreme boredom and alienation in the novels. He describes the upper-class suburban environment of his youth as dull, empty, lifeless, and vaguely hostile. Burroughs perceived early that the dullness of bourgeois life is not harmless, but is rather a positive evil resulting from the repression of sexuality and the oppression of the lower classes. The evil of dullness is embodied in the character of Colonel Greenfield in *The Wild Boys,* a great bore known for his interminable racist jokes. The child of the later novels is a timid, awkward, sensitive boy who strikes his elders as unwholesome and who feels himself to be an alien. Homosexuality is acknowledged but is not seen as the cause of his sense of difference. Often solitary, the child in *Junkie* turns to extensive reading, including Wilde, Baudelaire, Gide, and the autobiography of a burglar. Inspired by his reading, he indulges in outlaw fantasies and small criminal gestures. In the two later novels, the boy reads pulp magazines and dreams of becoming a writer. His first story is called "The Autobiography of a Wolf," reflecting his identification with the outlaw. He visits the courthouse on Saturdays to observe criminal trials, and admires the self-possessed, fearless attitude of two black men—father and son—who maintain their integrity before a hostile white judge. Feeling even more of an outsider as an adolescent, the boy of *Junkie* forms a romantic friendship with another boy, is rejected, and remains socially isolated. In the "Literary Autobiography," a fictionalized account of himself that repeats much of the same narrative as the novels, Burroughs tells of the diary he kept of his teenage romance, of his revulsion against the falsity of what he had written, and his destruction of the diary. He claims he then gave up writing until 1938.

Thus Burroughs presents his "childhood of the artist" in the postromantic tradition of alienation from bourgeois society. The French influence is apparent in his reading, while popular literature gives an American cast to the boy's conception of the outlaw. The boy who feels like an outsider finds models in the criminal and the artist, who are both seen as professional outsiders—not by choice but by social necessity.[16]

From 1932 to 1936 Burroughs attended Harvard University, where he continued to feel like an outsider, rejecting the (to him) pretentious social and educational environment. According to the preface of *Junkie,* he was

not interested in joining Harvard's homosexual set as a solution to his iso-
lation. Apparently he did not continue to write and has insisted in interviews that as a young adult he had no thoughts of becoming a writer. He
did, however, major in English literature; and T. S. Eliot, an important
influence in his fiction, lectured at Harvard while Burroughs was an un-
dergraduate. During his college years he must have begun his reading of
the modern authors whom he already knew so well when he became the
teacher of Ginsberg and Kerouac. But Burroughs has never attributed any
influence, literary or otherwise, to his schooling.[17]

After graduating from Harvard in 1936, Burroughs began receiving an
allowance from his parents and was free to do as he pleased. His own description of the following years is one of aimless drifting and boredom. But
a close look at his wanderings reveals an underlying quest that can only be
called spiritual.

The Hipster

Little is known about Burroughs's life from 1936 to 1944, a period in
which he attempted a number of conventional alternatives: medical school
in Vienna, graduate school in anthropology at Harvard, military service
(he was discharged after a few months), psychoanalysis, odd jobs including
ad-man, bartender, and exterminator in Chicago and New York City.[18] He
also continued his education in his own way by reading modern literature,
philosophy, and psychology, and by close observation of the various social
milieus he experienced. He began his lifelong practice of taking "observer's
notes" on specific social environments and their inhabitants, a habit that
may have been inspired by his anthropological studies. Although these
years have the appearance of aimlessness and although Burroughs portrays
himself in *Junkie* as a dilettante insulated from necessity by his private
income, his first novel also shows that a search was taking place for a reality
that would form the basis of a vocation, a morality, and a life-style—all of
which began to come together for him in his thirties.

While at Harvard in 1938, Burroughs began writing in collaboration
with an old friend from St. Louis, Kells Elvins. Together they wrote detective stories in the hardboiled style of Dashiell Hammett and Raymond
Chandler.[19] They also composed a short satire on the sinking of the *Titanic*
called "Twilight's Last Gleaming," which was rejected by *Esquire* and other
magazines but later included in *Nova Express*.[20] The writing with Elvins
foreshadows Burroughs's future style as a novelist: the ironic, "factual"
style of *Junkie* and the satirical fantasy of *Naked Lunch*. The *Titanic* piece

also marks the first appearance of Dr. Benway, a major character in several novels. The creation of Dr. Benway in 1938 and the subsequent incorporation of "Twilight's Last Gleaming" into a novel in 1964 indicates that Burroughs's characteristic themes and style were formed early, even though he did not begin a serious career as a writer until he was thirty-five. Creation through collaboration is also characteristic of Burrough's future practice as a writer. When his 1938 piece was rejected by publishers, Burroughs was discouraged from pursuing writing as a career, and did not try again for many years.[21]

The years of wandering constituted a long apprenticeship to his vocation as a writer, which paralleled his search for a belief to provide the basis for his life. That quest found its end in 1944 when Burroughs became a morphine addict. The life-style and values of the addict fulfilled Burroughs's yearning to identify himself with an outlaw group of men whose every daily action was an affront to the bourgeois social order. Furthermore, addiction ended dilettantism and gave a prophetic vision that enabled Burroughs to turn his life into art.

Burroughs was one of the first to perceive that "hipsterism," the special viewpoint of the addict underworld, would become the weltanschauung of postwar America—the "American existentialism" so brilliantly outlined several years later by Norman Mailer in his essay "The White Negro."[22] In fact, the "philosophical psychopath" defined by Mailer is in many ways an accurate description of Burroughs's attitude.

The hipster, says Mailer, is a man who rejects the social order of the modern bureaucratic state, which had its genesis in World War II. The hipster rejects not only the rules of behavior and the corresponding system of beliefs that the state imposes upon its members, but also the very self that this society shapes within the individual. The hipster seeks to create a new self that is free from external conditioning by living the economic life of a "marginal man" and by obeying his inner, nonrational impulses. He returns to infantile sexual and aggressive drives and the infantile wish for instant gratification in an attempt to find the roots of the unconditioned self and to make a new self free from social controls. Thus he becomes a psychopath by deliberate moral choice and with a philosophical program. The hipster conducts his life as a quest for alternative values and forms of the self. What makes the hipster different from other spiritual seekers is that his quest proceeds through action, not contemplation; and his radical program encompasses sex and violence, or, in Mailer's terms, orgasm and murder.

The hipster lives in a fluid social and psychological world in which only the present exists, in which the individual is a "vector in a network of forces,"[23] and in which context alone determines action. No a priori beliefs or rules govern behavior, but only the perception of the present context and the will to act upon that perception. The self is constantly changing in response to the context and the actions of the self, which help to create the context: self and world are a dynamic field of forces in which there are no fixed entities, only relationships. Reality is not dominated by matter, but by energy. The self is defined from moment to moment by choice and action. Thus the hipster is amoral by conventional standards, although he adheres to an exquisite standard of perception, honesty, and courage. The hipster is also a nihilist, but, as Mailer has pointed out, a basic affirmation underlies his negation of the social order: ". . . the nihilism of Hip proposes as its final tendency that every social restraint and category be removed, and the affirmation implicit in the proposal is that man would then prove to be more creative than murderous and so would not destroy himself."[24]

As Bruce Cook has observed in *The Beat Generation,* Mailer deemphasized the fact that drugs were the basis of hipsterism,[25] and instead focused on the psychopathic behavior of delinquent youth and the subculture of the Negro as the sources of hipsterism. Mailer's own artistic obsessions with salvation through sex and violence may have caused him to dismiss drug experiences as a form of the hipster's quest, but the omission in his essay may also reflect the date of its composition. By the time Mailer was writing, the hipster of the 1940s was disappearing and had passed his drug culture on to black jazz musicians, who, in turn, were transmitting "hip" values to middle-class white youth.

Burroughs's first novel, *Junkie,* a portrait of the addict underworld of the 1940s, reveals the true source of hipsterism, which the Mailer essay obscures, and the novel should be read as a corrective to "The White Negro." "Addict" and "hipster" are interchangeable terms in *Junkie.* The addict's's special angle of vision and way of life are the subject of the book. Seeing and living are one: the hipster's consciousness created by drugs. Burroughs calls the junkie's vision his "kick," and comments at the end of his novel that the vision is a permanent alteration of consciousness that remains even when drugs are given up: "You see things different when you return from junk."[26] *Junkie's* glossary of "jive talk," the argot of the addict underworld, is more extensive than the hip vocabulary discussed by Mailer. Mailer, for example, does not discuss the meaning of "kick" and does not reveal the addict origin of the term "beat."

The drug culture has been an important part of all "hip" and "beat" attitudes from the 1940s to the present. The social rebellion of white, middle-class "beatniks" and "hippies" was partly fueled by the alternative consciousness of drug experiences: hence, Burroughs's legendary status as an early leader in a widespread social movement—a leader in the sense that he took a path alone that many others would later follow.

And perhaps the aura of legend clings to him as well because he has written about an exotic American folk culture that now no longer exists. Burroughs was first introduced to morphine by Herbert Huncke, a Times Square hustler and addict, who fascinated him with his amorality and sophistication, his stories about the criminal underworld he inhabited, and his special language.[27] Through Huncke, the hipster, Burroughs became acquainted with an outlawed subculture that provided him with the images for his novels. In the *Paris Review* interview with Conrad Knickerbocker he calls it "the carny world" of old-time thieves and pickpockets and mentions the detailed notes he has kept about them.[28] The carny world provided Burroughs with characters, images, settings—a whole alternative world to the dominant social order that informs Burroughs's fiction from his first novel to his current work.

The year of Burroughs's introduction to morphine was also the year he met Jack Kerouac and Allen Ginsberg, two young men who admired him and encouraged him to write. The meeting of Burroughs, Kerouac, and Ginsberg in 1944 was the beginning of the Beats as a literary and social movement, although none of them would publish anything for years, and they certainly had no consciousness of having founded a group or a movement. They were simply friends with common interests and attitudes, particularly a rejection of an increasingly repressive American society, a quest for alternative values and life-styles, and, for the two younger men, a dream of becoming great writers together—a belief held with such youthful enthusiasm that Burroughs's own ambition was rekindled.

About ten years older than Kerouac and Ginsberg, Burroughs played the role of teacher as well as friend. He introduced them to modern literature and contemporary avant-garde thought as well as the underworld of petty criminals and addicts he had been exploring. Ginsberg has stated many times that Burroughs was his "greatest teacher"[29] and credits Burroughs with first introducing him to modern literature and modern ideas.[30] Kerouac's portraits of Burroughs in his novels, especially *On the Road,* show his admiration for the man and his continuing influence.[31] The authors Burroughs was reading and recommending at the time were an index to his own interests, and their influence can be seen in his fiction later on: eccentric system-builders Spengler, Korzybski, and Reich; Yeats of *A Vision;* European fiction by Céline, Kafka, and Gogol; modern poets T. S. Eliot, Yeats, Crane, and Auden; romantic rebels Blake, Rimbaud, and Cocteau; and popular writers Raymond Chandler, John O'Hara, and James M. Cain.[32]

But the younger men influenced Burroughs as well. In the generation of the 1940s, more than in his own peers, he found minds in sympathy with his own disaffection and quest for alternative experiences. Whereas he introduced them to underworld society, Ginsberg and Kerouac drew him into a younger (Columbia) university crowd that included his future wife. Furthermore, they urged him to write, particularly about his drug experiences. From 1944 on Burroughs kept in touch with and often shared living quarters with Ginsberg, Kerouac, and their mutual friends. Their debts to each other have been acknowledged again and again.

Burroughs has always said that Kerouac's belief in him as a writer was crucial,[33] and Ginsberg was instrumental in obtaining the publication of his early work. Burroughs and Kerouac collaborated in 1944 on a (never-published) novel, "And the Hippos Were Boiled in Their Tanks," each writing alternate chapters in Dashiell Hammett style about a murder based on the Carr/Kammerer case, in which Burroughs and Kerouac were involved as material witnesses.[34] In the early 1950s Burroughs mailed chapters of *Junkie* to Ginsberg as they were written, and Ginsberg succeeded in selling the manuscript to Ace Books, beginning his role as "literary agent" for his friends.[35] In 1953 Burroughs mailed to Ginsberg a series of letters that became "In Search of Yage," and from 1953 to 1957 he mailed portions of *Naked Lunch* to Ginsberg. In the late 1950s Kerouac typed up part of the *Naked Lunch* manuscript and gave the book its title.[36] Ginsberg first took the manuscript to Olympia Press in Paris, helped to get portions published by the *Black Mountain Review,* the *Chicago Review,* and *Big Table,* and acted as intermediary between Burroughs and Grove Press when the American edition was being prepared for publication. In 1960 Gregory Corso, whom Burroughs met through Ginsberg, collaborated with Burroughs, Sinclair Beiles, and Brion Gysin on *Minutes To Go,* an experiment with cutup poetry. In 1963 *The Yage Letters* was published, consisting of "In Search of Yage" by Burroughs and later texts by both Burroughs and Ginsberg. No doubt Ginsberg's friendship with Lawrence Ferlinghetti of City Lights Press, the publisher of *Howl,* led to the publication of *The Yage Letters.* These collaborations are an indication of significant influence, especially at the beginning of Burroughs's literary career.

Although Burroughs, Kerouac, and Ginsberg are very different artists, each with his own highly individual style and subject matter, they do share some themes and techniques that help to define the Beats as a literary and social movement. All three found conventional American society wanting in spiritual values and portray a quest for an alternative source of value. (Kerouac and Ginsberg maintain a belief in a transcendent reality, while Burroughs does not.) All three sought to expand consciousness through travel, sex, drugs, and new literary forms. All three knew Herbert Huncke and were influenced by his hipsterism. The technique of improvisation is important to all three writers, although only Kerouac made it his primary method of composition. Juxtaposition is an important technique for both Ginsberg and Burroughs, and both use it to create new insight. Finally, all three men fictionalized their own lives in their art and thus created an autobiographical myth. With the publication of *Howl, On the Road,* and *Naked Lunch* within a few years of each other, the three men collaborated in the creation of the legend of the Beat Generation.

The year of 1944 was the crucial juncture in Burroughs's life. As Burroughs remarked in the *Paris Review* interview, "after I became addicted in New York in 1944, things began to happen."[37] Drugs, friendship, and writing became his permanent occupations. He also started a family. In 1944 he met Joan Vollmer Adams, a friend of Edie Parker, Kerouac's first wife. She became his common-law wife in 1945, and William, Jr., was born in 1947. Joan Burroughs's daughter by a previous marriage also lived with them. Soon after their marriage they set up a household, in Texas and later in Louisiana, which was a parody of the American family with a junkie father, a benzedrine-addicted mother, a homestead whose main cash crop was marijuana, and other social dropouts as frequent visitors. But what was a bizarre life-style in the late 1940s would become quite common twenty years later. Many young rebels in postwar America, seeking an alternative to middle-class society, have, like Burroughs, chosen the hip life-style of the drug culture. Burroughs's family life, chronicled by Kerouac in *On the Road,* became part of a legend and a prophecy of things to come.

The Addict

For fifteen years Burroughs chose drug addiction as a way of life. The physical rhythms of his existence were governed by the addiction-with-drawal syndrome, and his movements were determined by legal difficulties and the availability of drugs. Threatened with arrest, he left New York for a farm in New Waverley, Texas. After an arrest for drunken driving in

Texas he moved to Algiers, Louisiana, across the Mississippi River from downtown New Orleans. In 1949 he was arrested for possession of illegal firearms and narcotics and fled to Mexico City before he was brought to trial. The atmosphere and laws in Mexico were more relaxed, and Mexico City was becoming a haven for American hipsters, many of them ex-GIs attending classes at Mexico City College, like Burroughs, who studied Aztec and Mayan archaeology. But social freedom was balanced by an increasing sense of bondage to morphine and the horrors of self-imposed withdrawal treatments.[38] The nightmare of physical deterioration reached a climax when Burroughs accidentally shot and killed his wife.[39] Forced to leave Mexico in 1952 as a result of the shooting, Burroughs first traveled to Tangier and South America, visited Ginsberg in New York in the fall of 1953, when they worked on "In Search of Yage," then settled in Tangier at the end of that year. His son went to live with Burroughs's parents, and Burroughs began to live the life of an expatriate writer. By 1954 he had published his first novel, *Junkie,* and had continued to develop his craft through recording his own experiences and observations and by creating satirical fantasies.

Although Burroughs argues persuasively about the lack of choice involved in addition to opiates, it is clear that he chose this fate. Addiction became his spiritual discipline as an artist. Burroughs used addiction for two purposes: deconditioning and expansion of consciousness. First, addiction could strip him of the past, social constraints, and the ego formed by those influences: the goal in this reductive process is psychic autonomy. Second, exploration of consciousness through drug-induced states could give new insights into mind and reality and produce new literary forms. Burroughs has been particularly interested in the realm of the irrational and the repressed—what he calls the world of dream.[40] These purposes led him to sample every mind-altering drug known to man, another legendary practice that gave him the reputation of "connoisseur of drugs."[41] *Junkie,* "In Search of Yage," and *Naked Lunch* are accurate reports of drug experiences; and Burroughs has written several articles on the effects of drugs, most notably "Letter from a Master Addict to Dangerous Drugs"[42] and "Points of Distinction between Sedative and Consciousness-expanding Drugs."[43]

But since narcotics addiction was necessarily his primary drug experience, Burroughs's ultimate vision of self and universe is a negative one. As an addict Burroughs found mental freedom in a drug that also produced physical bondage and social victimization. His life had been reduced to a basic contradiction—the duality of mind and body—which is the human condition. The extremity of Burroughs's experience had finally revealed that his fate was Everyman's, and the intensity of his vision gave the impetus for a series of novels in which Burroughs's experience is used as the basis for a mythology of modern man.

But none of these works could have been written by Burroughs the addict, for, as he has pointed out, opiates decrease awareness and thus the ability to write creatively.[44] In fact, Burroughs has denied that anything of worth can be written under the influence of any drug (with the possible exception of marijuana), although drugs may be useful for opening up psychic areas to be written about afterwards.[45] By 1956 Burroughs had published only *Junkie,* a reportorial narrative that did not demand great imaginative powers. Over the years he had compiled a mass of fragmentary notes containing drug and travel experiences and satirical fantasies attacking social ills. He has stated that he had about a thousand pages of notes out of which came *Naked Lunch* and the three subsequent novels.[46] But in 1957 he was practically immobilized by his drug habit. Filled with a sense of imminent death and, very possibly, the ambition to do something with his notes, he underwent the apomorphine cure of Dr. John Yerbury Dent of London. The cure was a success, and Burroughs became a proselytizer for apomorphine. (There were relapses, but Burroughs was completely cured by 1959.) As he remarked to Daniel Odier, "[apomorphine was] the turning point between life and death. I would never have been cured without it. *Naked Lunch* would never have been written."[47]

The Writer

From 1957 to the present Burroughs has devoted himself to writing. Literature has taken over the role that drugs once played in his life, and Burroughs has often called himself a "writing addict" in his work and in interviews. "Writing is more of a habit than using," he jokes repeatedly as a refrain in *The Soft Machine, The Ticket That Exploded,* and *Nova Express.* Thus, like many writers, Burroughs lives quietly, devoting himself to his work and seeing only a few close friends and collaborators. A very private and reserved person, he often employs his friends to act as intermediaries with his publishers and the public.

Burroughs remains a traveler, however, and his literary career seems to have provided the impetus for movement and change once provided by drugs. His travels and changes in residence for the past twenty-five years have been in response to his needs and opportunities as a writer, and Burroughs often portrays his movements as simply responses to external stimuli in the same way that he explains his drug addiction. Like many other expatriate writers, he has sought inexpensive and tolerant environments where other writers and artists have gathered, and the encouragement of publishers and friends has often precipitated the decision to move. His travels have put him in touch with the international avant-garde, especially with younger artists, and have given him an international reputation. At the same time, his long residence abroad, his personal reserve, and the autobiographical nature of his fiction have contributed to the creation of a Burroughs legend. This section summarizes the external events of Burroughs's life from the late 1950s to the present. The most important events, however, are the works and the evolution of his artistic technique and philosophy—the subject of the succeeding chapters.

One of the reasons Burroughs moved to Tangier was the availability of morphine, but he was also aware of the exotic city's colony of expatriate artists. He met Paul and Jane Bowles, and Paul introduced him in 1957 to Brion Gysin, a British-American painter who has been an important friend and literary influence. Burroughs also met Tennessee Williams and Terry Southern in Tangier and was visited by Ginsberg, Ansen, Peter Orlovsky, Gregory Corso, and Ian Sommerville—all of whom have been important friends and collaborators. Burroughs's residence in Tangier, the Villa Muniria, became a point of contact for other writers and artists and became affectionately known as the "Villa Delirium" in Beat Legend. It was in Tangier that *Naked Lunch* was written, as well as much of the material that went into the trilogy that followed. Burroughs has stated that by 1957 the writing of *Naked Lunch* was completed and that the collaboration with others took place in the editing process from 1957 to 1959.[48]

In 1958 Burroughs moved to Paris in order to be closer to his publisher, Maurice Girodias of Olympia Press. He lived at 9 Rue Git le Coeur, which became known as the "Beat Hotel" because of the writers and artists who passed through in the late 1950s and early 1960s. Sinclair Beiles, then an editor for Olympia Press, helped to edit the manuscript of *Naked Lunch* at the Beat Hotel and became a friend and collaborator. Gysin also moved to Paris in 1958, lived at the same address, and began his close collaborations with Burroughs. Girodias described Gysin as Burroughs's chief intermediary with his publisher at that time.[49] While he and Burroughs were living at the Beat Hotel, Gysin discovered the cutup technique, which had a major influence on Burroughs's art of the 1960s. Burroughs's first cutup experiments and cutup collaborations with Gysin, Beiles, and Corso took place in 1959, and the results were first published in Paris and San Francisco in 1960. From 1960 to 1964, Burroughs lived mostly in Paris, where Olympia Press published *The Soft Machine* and *The Ticket That Exploded* soon after bringing out *Naked Lunch.*

During the early 1960s Burroughs also stayed in London and Tangier on extended visits. He was partially drawn to London by his British publisher, John Calder, who began orchestrating Burroughs's introduction to the English public. Calder published *Naked Lunch* and *Dead Fingers Talk,* contributing quite a bit of editorial work on the latter, a compilation of pieces found in *Naked Lunch, The Soft Machine,* and *The Ticket That Exploded* that has never been reprinted.[50] These works provoked a notable review in the Times Literary Supplement and a lengthy exchange of letters on Burroughs.[51] Calder also arranged for Burroughs to attend the Edinburgh Writers Conference in 1962, where *Naked Lunch* was praised by Norman Mailer and Mary McCarthy, thus attracting widespread attention to Burroughs's work for the first time in Great Britain and the United States. Burroughs was also attracted to London by his friendships with Michael Portman and Ian Sommerville, who collaborated with him on tape-recorder and computer cutups—some of which were incorporated into the trilogy, and with Antony Balch, an experimental filmmaker who made three films with Burroughs and whose film experiments are also recorded in the trilogy and later works. While in Great Britain Burroughs became interested in Scientology, attended training sessions in London and Edinburgh, and incorporated some of these experiences in his fiction of the 1960s.

Burroughs spent part of 1961 in Tangier, where he was visited by Ginsberg, Orlovsky, Corso, Ansen, and Sommerville; and he completed *Nova Express,* the final novel of the trilogy, in Tangier in 1964. Imagery drawn from the Tangerian milieu is an important element in the trilogy and may have been part of the reason that Burroughs made return visits. His American friends kept him in touch with his native culture, so much a part of his worldview, voice, and style. One notable contact between Burroughs and the counterculture in the United States at that time was his meeting with Timothy Leary in 1961. Ginsberg, who had previously participated in some of Leary's drug experiments, arranged for Burroughs to travel to Harvard to ingest psilocybin under Leary's observation. The meeting was not a success: Burroughs returned from the trip declaring Leary to be "the most unscientific man I ever met."[52]

Burroughs returned to the United States in 1965 in order to visit and write about his birthplace for the *Evergreen Review.* He was interviewed there by Conrad Knickerbocker for the *Paris Review,* which also published parts of his St. Louis scrapbook of cutups. This interview is an index of his impact upon the literary scene of the early 1960s and is highly informative about his themes and techniques at the time. After living in New York City for the remainder of 1965, Burroughs settled in London for several years because London provided an inexpensive and congenial environment for his work. Gysin also moved to London and continued to work with Burroughs, as did Sommerville and Balch. According to Bockris, Ian Sommerville became Burroughs's closest companion and collaborator in the late 1960s.[53] But Burroughs maintained his ties with Parisian writers as well: Daniel Odier and Philippe Mikriamos interviewed Burroughs and published important books on his work.[54]

During the late 1960s Burroughs concentrated on multimedia experiments with his collaborators. Barry Miles has stated that much of the work was unpublishable,[55] and Burroughs and Gysin discussed their publishing difficulties in the Palmer interview. Burroughs did, however, publish many short pieces in underground literary and political journals in England, the United States, France, Germany, and elsewhere. His work also appeared in many anthologies, and he gave many interviews. These publications put Burroughs in touch with younger writers—most significantly, Miles, who became Burroughs's bibliographer; Jeff Nuttal, editor of *My Own Mag,* which published much Burroughs material in the 1960s; Graham Masterson, editor of *Mayfair,* which published the Academy Series; Claude Pélieu and Mary Beach, his French translators and collaborators; and Carl Weissner, a German collaborator. Through his friends Burroughs also met several rock music stars (among them Mick Jagger, Paul McCartney, and David Bowie) and was introduced to the youth culture of the 1960s. He was interviewed twice by *Rolling Stone,* which served to link him to the current rock scene in the mind of the public. In 1968 he attended the Democratic National Convention in Chicago as a reporter for *Esquire* and observed firsthand the protest movement against the Vietnam War. These contacts with the generation of the 1960s put Burroughs in touch with the politics of the youth revolt, providing new materials for his future fictions. He made many sympathetic statements about youthful rebellion in his work and in interviews, leading many readers to believe that he had become politically active.[56] But his life remained devoted to private artistic exploration with a few close friends. He neither joined nor led any political organizations, and he has remarked in a recent interview that the turmoil of the 1960s was a cultural, not a political revolt.[57] But Burroughs's contacts with the youth culture did give him new themes and images for his fiction. In fact, his work from *The Wild Boys* (1971) to the present has as its initial inspiration the youth revolt of the 1960s.

Because of his links with younger artists and rebels, Burroughs's legend continued to grow. For American youth, the expatriate Burroughs was a remote and mysterious figure known only through his work and that of Kerouac and Ginsberg. He was the "Beat Godfather"[58] or the "Holy Monster."[59] In England and Europe he was perceived within the context of current avant-garde art. Younger artists imitated his methods, appropriated his images, collaborated with him, and published their work alongside his. Through association with new art, Burroughs maintained a reputation as an outsider and artist of revolt. British critic, Eric Mottram, placed Burroughs in a radical aesthetic and political context in *William Burroughs: The Algebra of Need*—the first full-length study of Burroughs's work in English.[60]

In 1974 Burroughs moved to New York City at the suggestion of Ginsberg, who arranged for Burroughs to teach a creative-writing course at the City College of New York that spring and to lecture in the summers at the Jack Kerouac School of Disembodied Poetics, part of the Naropa Institute in Boulder, Colorado. Summers in Colorado also enabled Burroughs to visit his son there until the son's death in 1981. Burroughs settled in New York and, soon after his arrival, met James Grauerholz, who became his companion, secretary, and agent. Since returning to the United States, he has lectured, given readings, and published much old and new work. In 1978 a "Nova Convention" was held in New York from 30 November to 2 December. It consisted of lectures, films, exhibitions, and performances in honor of William S. Burroughs. Many avant-garde writers, artists, and musicians participated, testifying to Burroughs's widespread influence among younger artists. In 1981 Burroughs published his first long fiction in several years, *Cities of the Red Night,* the chief result of his collaboration with Grauerholz. In 1983 Burroughs was inducted into the American Academy and Institute of Arts and Letters.

The Legend

Burroughs's biography has become a legend in the tradition of the post-romantic artist. The legendary career is one we all recognize as that of the *Künstlerroman* and the *poète maudit*. The life of the artist that emerges from Burroughs's fiction and from his public "image" can be summarized as follows.

As a child the artist feels alienated from his bourgeois surroundings, but the source of that alienation is mysterious and elusive. He early identifies

himself with other "outsiders"—the artist and the criminal—and the two
are linked in his mind as he begins to write as a child. In adolescence, the
artist's alienation intensifies as he finds that his sexuality deviates from the
bourgeois norm. Homosexuality is also linked in his mind to criminal and
artistic behavior. As a young adult the artist wanders through his society,
postponing career and marriage while conducting a quest for self, belief,
and vocation. The quest is conducted through experience, and the artist
seeks out extreme experiences and psychic states so as to explore life fully.
He is particularly attracted to forbidden experiences: sex, drugs, and
crime. He intends by his behavior to shock the bourgeoisie at the same
time as he truly seeks his salvation. His quest may, like Burroughs's, include literal geographical travel, and he may choose to act out his alienation by expatriation. Frequently, like Burroughs, the artist finds his
ultimate reality in the ultimate depravity that is hell for him. (In Burroughs's case drug addiction is this experience.) But the artist survives his
journey through hell and returns to normal society with a vison, a new,
mature self, and an artistic vocation. He conveys his private vision to others through art and becomes an oracle, a prophet, and a guru. The son-
figure becomes a father-figure to younger artists or to youth in general. In
his iconoclastic art, the artist struggles to keep the vision alive, and his art
is itself a constant renewal of visionary experience. He plays the role of
permanent rebel and leader of the avant-garde.

     This is the shape Burroughs has given to his biography in his writing
and in interviews. Kerouac and Ginsberg also made use of the same mythic
pattern in their art and in their homage to Burroughs. The legend has also
been elaborated upon by admirers and the popular media. This legend has
given Burroughs many heroic epithets: connoisseur of drugs, master addict, mad genius, Beat guru, holy monster, Beat godfather, cosmonaut of
inner space, and mythmaker of the space age. And this is the legend the
critic must evaluate as a significant part of Burroughs's literary career.

     For the legend is integral to Burroughs's art. As a hipster Burroughs
was a philosophical psychopath, and as a hip artist he is a theoretician-
writer who defines a new aesthetic while creating literary artifacts. Burroughs's aesthetic—the Beat aesthetic—is one that defines art as a consciousness. For Burroughs, the perceptions that become literature are as
much an aesthetic experience as the words on the page; experience and
narration of experience are both creative acts and equally "real." The hip
principles of honesty, clarity, spontaneity, and improvisation dictate that
autobiography is the only literature. And recording one's consciousness as
vision or story is to create legend.

Art as a mode of consciousness, then, is a continual, developing process indistinguishable from the artist's life. What gives unity to experiences and individual works is the single mind that produced them. The novels that result from this aesthetic are fragmentary, but the legendary career of the man emerges from the total artistic activity as a unified, structured whole made up of life *and* works, and perhaps this is the only view of Burroughs that can give a true appreciation of his art. The works must be seen in relation to the legend of the artist as rebel, seeker, prophet, and innovator. An American predecessor in this mode of art and legend is Walt Whitman, whose *Leaves of Grass* also creates a legend of the author in an attempt to create a new mythology.[61] The analogy with Whitman shows Burroughs's links with the American literary tradition as well as the modern avant-garde with its center in Paris. The chapters that follow show the evolution of Burroughs's art and his corresponding theory of art and examine how he unites biography and fiction into the art of consciousness.

Chapter Two
The Artist's Quest

Burroughs's career as a writer began at the age of thirty-five when he began to record his experiences as an addict. From about 1950 to 1957 he kept notes that included not only observations about the drug world and the effects of drugs on himself, but also records of dreams, memories, and fantasy episodes. Often this material was included in letters to his friends. From the beginning Burroughs wrote in fragments, recording all of the products of his consciousness, whether fact or fiction, "subjective" or "objective," and encouraged collaboration with other artists through letters, visits, and the mediation of others with his publishers. From the selection, editing, and arrangement of the notes came *Junkie, The Yage Letters, Naked Lunch, The Soft Machine, The Ticket That Exploded* and *Nova Express*—all of which are based on Burroughs's life as a drug addict.

The first three works form a sequence, showing how Burroughs learned to transform life into art and gradually discovered his individual style as a mature, avant-garde artist. *Junkie* and *The Yage Letters* present Burroughs's experiences in a straightforward narrative and an autobiograhical form. The "matter" of Burroughs's major work is contained in these early efforts, which also record a search for an appropriate fictional form. Using the material of the early novels in a new way in *Naked Lunch,* Burroughs found his characteristic form and style and broke the boundaries of conventional fiction. *Naked Lunch* is Burroughs's first mature work as an artist, the novel that established his reputation as an important writer and the one that still receives the most critical attention.

Addiction as Quest: *Junkie*

Early in 1950, while living in Mexico City, Burroughs began to write *Junkie,* sending the chapters in the mail to Ginsberg, who was then living with his family in Paterson, New Jersey.[1] When the book was completed, Ginsberg acted as Burroughs's agent and made the rounds of the publishers with the manuscript. He had no luck with the major publishing houses and was able to get the book accepted for paperback publication by Ace

Books in 1952 only through the personal friendship of Carl Solomon, who was the nephew of the owner. (Ginsberg had met Solomon during his stay in a mental institution in 1949 and later dedicated "Howl" to his fellow inmate.) Because of the "drug fiend" hysteria of the times, Burroughs was asked to write a prologue about his respectable family background, and a few passages and one whole section were arbitrarily cut.[2] Solomon wrote a placating introduction explaining that the book should be read as a warning, and parenthetical editor's notes were inserted "to indicate where the author clearly departs from accepted medical fact or makes other unsubstantiated statements in an effort to justify his actions."[3]

The novel was originally published in 1953 as a doubledecker paperback along with *Narcotic Agent* by Maurice Helbrant. As Ginsberg remarks, it was "a shabby package; on the other hand, given our naiveté, a kind of brave miracle that the text actually was printed and read over the next decade by a million cognoscenti."[4] But given Burroughs's interest in popular culture, the original form of publication must have appealed to his ironic sense of humor.

Largely ignored by the critics and dismissed as unimportant by Burroughs himself,[5] *Junkie* lays the groundwork for the later novels and is itself a complex work that deserves more attention than it has received, for it introduces many of Burroughs's continuing themes, characters, images, and settings. It also shows his early experimentation with form through the ironic use of conventions from popular literature.

Junkie records the experiences of William Lee as an "unredeemed" drug addict. The novel is autobiographical; but fact is transmuted into fiction through selection, arrangement, tone, and point of view. *Junkie* begins with Bill Lee's first introduction to morphine and his gradual drifting into addiction and involvement in the underworld of petty crime inhabited by most addicts. The addicts and their world are carefully described and analyzed. Plotless in the usual sense, the novel follows the adventures of the addict-narrator, recording his progress through the development of four drug "habits"; the subsequent withdrawals and cures; and his travels ever southward to evade trouble with the law. Descriptive and narrative episodes are interspersed with expository passages giving factual information about the drug world and reflective passages that attempt to generalize from personal experience. The conclusion of the novel provides no climax or resolution, suggesting a continuation of what has gone before as the narrator prepares to travel even farther South in search of a new drug that promises telepathic powers.

In a severely understated narrative, *Junkie* introduces the great theme that has been Burroughs's obsession as a writer: the quest. He portrays the search for an absolute that will give peace of mind and provide escape from a repulsive social world devoid of spiritual values. The quest is conducted through the nonrational means of drug addiction, which entails a withdrawal from the larger social world to an underground society with its own special terrain and terminology. Addiction also negates the usual bodily needs, awareness of physical surroundings, and the emotions accompanying bodily attachments to the external world. Freed from social and physical bonds, the addict acquires a special vision of reality, different from and perhaps more profound than the perceptions of ordinary consciousness. But the quest through drugs is an unending one, requiring more and more drugs, and *Junkie* ends with further flight, a search for a new drug and the new vision it can provide, implying that the only conclusion to the quest is death.

That the addiction of *Junkie*'s protagonist is a kind of interior quest is implied rather than stated. The curiously detached "I" of the novel avoids any extensive psychological description or analysis of motivation. Viewing the self from the outside, the narrator portrays his actions as unmotivated and aimless. He drifts from one situation to another, frequently changing associates, employment, living quarters, cities, and even countries. His movements seem to trace a pattern of flight and evasion determined by external physical forces—the availability of drugs and the pressure of the law. Yet a close reading of the novel reveals a spiritual quest that motivates the seemingly random movements and strict selection of material.

The preface of *Junkie,* an account of the protagonist Bill Lee's life before becoming an addict, indicates that Lee is not only fleeing but also exploring alternatives to life in the macrocosm—the conventional middle-class American social existence, which exacts lifeless conformity from its participants and which uses money to isolate and insulate them in the "comfortable capsules" of suburbia. Lee's childhood alienation from this milieu is expressed in bad dreams, reading decadent literature (Wilde, Baudelaire, Gide), and an early attraction to crime and homosexuality: "At this time I was greatly impressed by an autobiography of a burglar, called *You Can't Win*. The author claimed to have spent a good part of his life in jail. It sounded good to me compared with the dullness of a Midwest suburb where all contact with life is shut out. I saw my friend as an ally, a partner in crime" (J, p. 8).[6] Beginning with his youthful escapades, Lee is not only trying to evade entrapment by an oppressive society equated with death-in-life, but he is also searching for an alternative society or vision that will give him the feeling of being alive by overcoming alienation.

The university, the international homosexual set, the European tour or exile, graduate school, jiujitsu, psychoanalysis, the army, various jobs—none provides the special vision because Lee is still cut off from "real life" by his inheritance; money makes every effort unnecessary, superfluous (J, p. 9). He is first attracted to drugs as a form of crime that would make the safety of money irrelevant, but drugs produce a much more far-reaching result by eliminating the insulation of money. For the first time in his life, Lee needs money (J, p. 10). Furthermore, drug addiction becomes more than an attitude of rebellion: it promises vision. Addiction gives the most extreme states of pain and pleasure, need and fulfillment, tension and relaxation possible to the human organism. It bares the mainsprings of individual and social psychology. The preface ends with the lessons learned from addiction as "a way of life."

Although his goal is visionary, the protagonist's conduct of the quest is pseudoscientific. He approaches his new psychic and physical experiences like a scientific observer with the self as experimental subject. He records data about addiction and hypothesizes general laws on the basis of the data. Two aspects of addiction are described and analyzed: the society of addicts and the effects of drugs on the individual. The former leads to generalizations about society and its institutions; the latter, to a psychology of addiction.

The junk world of addicts, petty criminals, sexual deviants, police, lawyers, and doctors is peopled by grotesques warped by need and hypocrisy. Addicts and criminals are driven by physical and economic needs (the two are hardly separable to Burroughs) that the law attempts to thwart. Need distorts and simplifies both mind and body so that the person becomes a caricature with an underworld moniker that fixes his limited identity. The man in need is flat, one-dimensional, and often animal-like in appearance, a grotesque worthy of portrayal in a Dick Tracy comic strip. The attitude toward these characters is nonjudgmental; the narrator's point of view is that of a scientist describing the flora and fauna of a particular environment.

Burroughs's descriptions of underworld characters in *Junkie* show how he arrived at the characterizations of *Naked Lunch* and the later novels. When people are reduced and molded by need, their identities reside in their functions. Subway Mike, for example, *is* his profession: He "had a large, pale face and long teeth. He looked like some specialized kind of underground animal that preys on animals of the surface. He was a skillful lushworker, but he had no front. Any cop would do a doubletake at the sight of him, and he was well-known to the subway squad" (J, p. 26). Such superficial identities frequently shift and change with circumstances, and several characters undergo metamorphoses. For example, Jack, the successful thief, suffers from sudden and severe fluctuations in weight that make him unrecognizable to acquaintances (J, p. 20). Dupre, the addict, changes appearance markedly when he is on and off drugs (J, p. 96). Some characters are so absorbed by need that they have no identity at all: "There was not much left of Nick. His constant, unsatisfied hunger had burned out all other concerns" (J, p. 51). Lack of identity can be an advantage in the underworld. Bill Gains's "vague respectable presence," for example, is perfectly adapted to his work: stealing overcoats (J, p. 50).

Need and vice reduce many to the subhuman. Both "junkies" and "fags" are described as puppets because of their stylized gestures. Animal comparisons, however, are the most common element in the caricatures in *Junkie,* and the animals referred to always have negative connotations. Characters are compared to sheep, rats, pigeons, fish, buzzards, frogs, lizards, snakes, and insects, as well as just being called animal-like.

The insect image is most important; for Burroughs, the insect life-form is the most repulsive and hostile to man. The most degraded humans become insectlike, such as Doolie in the throes of withdrawal sickness (J, p. 62). The narrator's own worst withdrawal nightmares concern insects. While withdrawing from his first habit early in the book, he has a vision of New York in ruins, overrun by centipedes and scorpions (J, p. 39). In the nightmarish alcoholic withdrawal from his fourth habit near the end of the novel, Lee envisions a human face transformed into a "crustacean horror," an image that reflects his own deterioration from man to the site of horrors: "the final place where the human road ends" (J, p. 112). The metamorphosis downward from man to insect is Burroughs's most powerful image in *Junkie* of man taken over by needs and functions.

Sometimes the caricatures of *Junkie* lead to the portrayal of universal types of evil. Gene Doolie, for example, is portrayed as the typical informer: "He probably pulled out dirty lists of people—his hands were always dirty—and read them off to the law. You could see him bustling into Black and Tan headquarters during the Irish Trouble; in a dirty gray toga turning in Christians, giving information to the Gestapo; the GPU, sitting in a cafeteria talking to a narcotics agent" (J, p. 54). The factual classification of types can also become the basis for fantasy, as with the Near Eastern type always seen in junk neighborhoods: "He has the mark of a certain trade or occupation that no longer exists. . . . What is his lost trade? Definitely of a servant class and something to do with the dead, though he is not an embalmer. Perhaps he stores something in his body—a substance to prolong life—of which he is periodically milked by his masters. He is as specialized as an insect, for the performance of some inconceivably vile function" (J, pp. 99–100).

Members of the larger society who deal with the underworld in order to control it (police, lawyers, and doctors) are also grotesque caricatures. But because they hypocritically deny the need in themselves and others, they are subjected to satirical contempt. There are only two kinds of policemen, the "tough cop" and the "con cop." They are largely motivated by vicarious participation in vice. Doctors, contemptuously called "croakers," take a hypocritical attitude toward addiction, refusing to recognize it as an over-powering physical need yet profiting from it by writing illegal morphine prescriptions if given a plausible story. Their own economic need and hy-pocrisy make them a gallery of grotesques:

> There are several varieties of writing croakers. Some will write only if they are convinced you are an addict, others only if they are convinced you are not. . . . There was one oldtime doctor who lived in a Victorian brownstone in the West Seventies. With him it was simply necessary to present a gentlemanly front. . . . Another doctor was always drunk and it was a matter of catching him at the right time. . . . Still another doctor was senile, and you had to help him write the script. (J, pp. 33–34)

Doctors, especially psychiatrists, who try to treat addiction in institutional settings are mercilessly satirized because they refuse to recognize the phys-ical aspect of addiction and because their care for the sick disguises a sadis-tic need to control others. Dr. Fredericks, the New Orleans psychiatrist, is the most contemptible character in the book; he is a weak, stupid man who dominates the pathetic inmates of a mental institution with his view of psychic health (J, pp. 93–94).

The only authorities who are not satirized are doctors who "know the score" and lawyers. Doctors who recognize the physical need of addiction without hypocrisy are realistic inhabitants of the world of need. Lawyers always know the score, since they profit from crime and cynically manip-ulate judges, juries, and police. Lee's New Orleans lawyer, Tige, uses bribes and lies to free his clients. Like the criminal, he succeeds with luck, imagination, and cunning, and when that does not work he suggests leav-ing the country. The practice of law is just another underworld profession, one that is accepted by the larger society as well.

The inhabitants of the drug world are observed, recorded, classified, and generalized into types and symbols of abstract forces. The experience of addiction produces a different view of "character" in life and art from the conventional one. People are not seen as complex personalities but as the locus of external and internal forces that are impersonal.

The addict's milieu, "junk territory," is amorphous and shifting. Junk is found in disreputable transitional neighborhoods where the big world and the little world meet for mutual satisfaction, the underworld providing distasteful and illegal services to the respectable. All of the junkie's important transactions take place in crowded, seedy places, usually public: tenements, shabby hotels, bars, cafeterias, subways. The one thing that holds these anomalous areas together is the need for drugs. The milieu reflects the character of the inhabitants with its constantly shifting, faded identity, held together only by need. These images of junk neighborhoods are carried on into later works as the scene of ambiguous and sinister social-economic-sexual transactions. For Burroughs, junk territory is the modern city as Waste Land—the ruins of civilization devoured by its subhuman products.

Society's official attitude toward drugs and its attempt to control their use are also part of the addict's milieu. Jails and hospitals are the other public stages provided for his existence. They are seen simply as totalitarian environments run by men who need to exert power over others. The large amount of factual information about drug laws and law enforcement included in *Junkie* is used to show the irrationality of official policy and those who execute it. The junkie regards these officials and their institutions merely as adversaries to be outwitted in a predatory social order. The portrayal of the sadistic power relationship between the authorities and addicts is the basis for Burroughs's analysis of power in the later novels.

The individual's subjective drug experience in *Junkie* is also described by Lee in a detached, objective manner, even though he himself is the guinea pig. A striking fact of this reportage is that addiction is almost always described as painful and revolting because withdrawal is portrayed more frequently than getting high. The novel offers a literal explanation of this pattern when Lee reflects, "When you look back over a year on the junk, it seems like no time at all. Only the periods when you were sick stand out. You remember the first few shots of a habit and the shots when you were really sick" (J, pp. 105–6).

The pleasant physical sensation given by a shot of morphine is described only once—when the protagonist takes his first shot at the beginning of the novel (J, p. 23). This "wave of relaxation," however, is immediately followed by a negative mental reaction: a feeling of fear accompanied by threatening images and a sense of impending death. From the very first, addiction is associated with death, and pleasure is quickly followed by suffering. Only two other mildly pleasant experiences are described: the bittersweet pain of mild withdrawal symptoms, which arouses childhood memories (J, p. 107), and the controlled excitement of anticipation during the ritual of preparation (J, p. 118). The former instance is cut off by a new injection, again equated with death. The second episode is suffused with irony since Lee is returning to addiction after a long period of painful withdrawal and abstinence.

Withdrawal symptoms provide a host of images of the body as ugly, vile, and weak. The most striking image is the withdrawal orgasm, associated with the orgasm of the hanged man. The novel ends with a nightmarish withdrawal episode, which lasts for weeks and creates a hell of alcoholism, physical deterioration, "uncontrollable sociability" (*sic*), emotional binges, paranoia, hostility, and violence. Finally, Lee nearly dies of uremic poisoning. The scenes describing Lee's irrational behavior are horrific even though Burroughs maintains the usual restrained tone.

It is during this final withdrawal period that Lee makes the sole subjective comments that appear in the book about his physical condition, thus alerting the reader to the seriousness of his plight. He says he had a "terrible feeling of helplessness" when he failed to kick his habit (J, p. 106); he feels pity for his violated body (J, p. 107); he admits he has "deteriorated shockingly" (J, p. 108). Burroughs also allows other characters to comment on Lee's deterioration for the first time in the book. Yet, soon after his recovery, Lee becomes addicted again and the cycle continues. The drug experience begins and ends with the insinuation that junk is death, "the static horror."

The factual description of addiction is accompanied by attempts to outline general laws about the nature of the experience, and Burroughs begins to create in *Junkie* his own pseudoscience of addiction. Junk is defined as "a way of life" that absorbs the total person. The very cells of one's body become committed to junk, and quitting is a "cellular decision," not a moral one. The special pleasure or "kick" of junk *is* the total subjection to junk. Addiction also gives the kick of a special angle of vision. At the end of the novel Lee says, "Like a man who has been away for a long time, you see things different when you return from junk" (J, p. 125). The protagonist of *Junkie* claims to have learned many things from his addiction: that life is pain, that all pleasure is relief and thus that the only complete pleasure is death, that there is a void at the center of the human personality, and that there is no escape except the momentary freedom of that special angle of vision.

The exploration of addiction in *Junkie* is used to call into question con-

ventional attitudes about the individual and society, mind and body. What
has been rejected by the dominant middle-class social order as deviating
from the norm is shown in *Junkie* as revealing the truth about the norm.
Deviant society—the "carny world"—mirrors the dominant society, exposing a predatory, amoral social order and individuals without "character"
or free will whose identities are wholly formed by needs and social functions. The addict's special angle of vision is the hipster mentality that en-
ables survival in this dangerous world.

The Originality of *Junkie*

The confessional novel form, which Burroughs uses to communicate the
negative quest of addiction, has both popular and literary antecedents,
and, superficially, *Junkie* seems to conform to the tradition. With its original subtitle, "The Confessions of an Unredeemed Drug Addict," its publication as a doubledecker paperback along with the memoirs of a narcotics
agent, and its hardboiled journalistic style, *Junkie* imitates the popular
confession of pulp magazines. Like the popular "true confession," *Junkie* is
a spare first-person narrative that deemphasizes introspection in favor of
action and the sensational details of crime and the criminal's world. Bill
Lee is a shallow persona who is hardly more than a vehicle for portraying
the immoral and secret underworld. But *Junkie* differs strikingly from the
popular confession in its amoral stance; this protagonist is pointedly "unredeemed," and the original publisher was squeamish enough about this
aspect of the work to include editorial disclaimers in a foreword and at
certain points in the book "for the protection of the reader."

The example of Rousseau might be cited as the forerunner of the more
literary, amoral confession, but *Junkie* differs from Rousseau's *Confessions,*
and the literary confession in general, in avoiding the subjective and emotional—the form's *raison d'être. Junkie* plays little attention to the inner life
and, indeed, seems to imply that it does not exist. Similarly, *Junkie* departs
from the more recent tradition of the confessional novel established by
Dostoevsky in *Notes from Underground,* Gide in *The Immoralist,* Sartre in
Nausea, and Camus in *The Fall,* although Burroughs's subject—alienation—is related to this convention. The fictional confession is, above all,
concerned with self and self-knowledge, like the true confession. Yet this
is where Burroughs radically departs from the confessional form, in spite
of the fact that the work is partly autobiographical.

The key to *Junkie*'s originality is the work's narrator-protagonist, the
persona "Bill Lee." This persona is and is not William S. Burroughs. He

has some of Burroughs's characteristics and life experiences, but not all of them; he is a much more limited and shallow personality than the author—a caricature of Burroughs as a drug addict. The persona impresses the reader as a nameless cipher because his name is rarely used and because of his lack of subjectivity. The "I" never gives any detailed account of his inner life, which we usually expect from a first-person narrator. Rather, his observations of persons, places, and events around him are recorded in a detached, objective manner with subjective reactions kept to a minimum. The narrator relates his own words and actions with the same detachment, and the only subjective experiences recorded are states of extreme pleasure and pain. Personal matters, such as the narrator's relationship with his wife, are simply omitted.

The "I" of *Junkie* is not a subject, but an object that is observed and recorded in interaction with other objects and physical forces as it passes through a series of life-experiences conceived of as scientific experiments. Burroughs was able to objectify a part of himself, which allowed him to get beyond the superficial level of the personality or ego to portray a more basic level of human existence—a level less personal but more powerful and enduring and ultimately more "real." On the other hand, the use of this kind of persona has a reductive and satirical effect. At times, Bill Lee seems comparable to the *picaro* of an eighteenth-century novel. Burroughs's picaresque addict can be compared to Defoe's Moll Flanders (whose confession is also ironic) and to Swift's Gulliver (whose travels to strange societies satirize his own society). Burroughs has himself commented on the picaresque form of his works.[7] His affinity for Swift becomes more overt in *Naked Lunch,* and in the recent *Cities of the Red Night* he imitates the eighteenth-century novel form.

The narrator's style is, as has been noted, impersonal, factual, and reportorial. Burroughs imitates the hardboiled reporter who conveys all the facts without bias or feeling, but with a cool, ironic superiority. This kind of reporter explores a "social problem" with sensational potential and portrays it by a combination of narrative and factual exposition—exactly the technique used in *Junkie.* Burroughs intersperses his narrative with expository passages giving factual information about the drug world: the physiological effects of various drugs, the symptoms of addiction and withdrawal, various kinds of withdrawal treatments, the descriptions of typical drug territory and typical inhabitants, the techniques of various criminals and conmen, a glossary of hip terms, federal and state narcotics laws, arrest and conviction procedures, a comparison of the drug policy in the United States with that of other countries, and the conventional journalistic conclusion summarizing the present state of affairs and listing the various solutions and their feasibility. The characterization of *Junkie* is the flat portraiture and caricature of journalism. Thus *Junkie* imitates the documentary style of journalism, but with the ironic twist that the entire story is told from the junkie's point of view rather than that of the "establishment." The junkie characterizes the present state of affairs in the United States as "nationwide hysteria," and the only good solution he can offer is to leave the country.

Junkie appears to be a plotless and rather formless work, the picaresque adventures of an underworld character, unified only by the presence of one major characer, one point of view, and one subject. But the underlying action of the unfulfilled quest provides a coherent plot and structure. The structure is based on the organic cycle of addiction-withdrawal, yearning and frustration. The formation of four habits is narrated, each one leading to a climax of trouble with the law and painful withdrawal. Each habit is stronger than the last, and the physical and legal consequences become more and more serious. The action based on this structure is an actual and symbolic flight to the South, where there is greater freedom in the use of drugs and sexuality but also greater horror at the void these vices reveal. Finally, the work ends on an inconclusive note, the cycle beginning again as the narrator prepares to head farther South. The open ending is expressive of the theme of unending flight and quest.

Junkie is a complex and ironic work, and it leaves the disturbing impression that the author has somehow tricked the reader into a realm where physical and social realities begin to shift and dissolve. Although its purposeful limitations deny this novel the power of the later works, *Junkie* provides the images and motifs of the subsequent novels—characters, places, scenes, episodes. And Burroughs's experimentation with form, especially his use of popular elements, is a preparation for an even more radical style in the future.

Further Travels: "In Search of Yage"

After leaving Mexico City in 1952, Burroughs embarked on a period of travel before settling in Tangier in 1954. He first decided to tour South America, ostensibly in search of yage, a hallucinogenic drug used by Colombian Indians. From January to July 1953, Burroughs wrote frequent letters to Ginsberg telling him about his trip. In the fall of 1953 Burroughs joined Ginsberg in New York City, and they proceeded to edit the letters for publication with the help of Aileen Lee and Alan Ansen as typists.[8] According to Ansen and Robert Creeley, the letters called "In Search of Yage" were originally part of a trilogy that included *Junkie* and *Queer,* a novel about homosexuality Burroughs wrote contemporaneously with *Junkie* and "In Search of Yage."[9] *Queer* has never been published, and the letters were not to be published for many years.

In 1959 *Big Table* printed several of the letters as a further introduction of the work of Burroughs to the public.[10] (They had previously published some episodes from *Naked Lunch,* the first appearance of that manuscript in the United States.) Finally, in 1963, ten years after it had been completed, "In Search of Yage" was published by City Lights as part of an "epistolary novel" called *The Yage Letters.* The book includes eleven letters from Burroughs to Ginsberg describing his search for yage from January to July 1953; a letter from Ginsberg to Burroughs written in 1960 describing Ginsberg's subsequent South American trip and yage experience; Burroughs's 1960 reply from London explaining the cutup method he had recently discovered; and an epilogue written in 1963, which includes a short note by Ginsberg, addressed "To whom it may concern," explaining his later interpretation of his yage visions, and a short piece by Burroughs called "I Am Dying, Meester?" which employs the cutup technique to create a collage from the materials in the earlier letters.

The "In Search of Yage" section of *The Yage Letters* is indeed an "epistolary novel," although a short one (about forty pages), which continues the quest described in *Junkie* by giving a fictionalized account of the further travels announced at the end of the first novel. Again, fiction is created from literal biography through selection and editing. The mode of composition (actual letters), the collaborative editing and publication, and the inclusion of later material in the 1963 book are all typical of Burroughs's practice as a writer. He refuses to conform to the convention of the final text produced by the individual artist.

The series of letters are like a coda to *Junkie,* carrying the action one step further but repeating the same theme. The same unending quest is followed with yage as the impetus rather than morphine; the same organic pattern of yearning, frustration, and flight is presented. The same protagonist conducts the quest: the letters are signed "Bill," "William," "Willy Lee," and "W. Lee." South America becomes the archetypal southern experience of freedom to satisfy the body with drugs and sex but with greater degradation and frustration as a result. Homosexuality becomes as prominent as drugs but equally disappointing. Cities and entire countries become archetypes of sinister decay, and the police become more intrusive and irrational as obstructions to individual gratification. Again, the quest is conducted in a pseudoscientific manner, the results are overwhelmingly negative, and the static horror of death lies at the end, resulting in another flight at the close of the narrative: "Suddenly I wanted to leave Lima right away. This feeling of urgency has followed me like my ass all over South America. . . . Where am I going in such a hurry? Appointment in Talara, Tingo Maria, Pucallpa, Panama, Guatemala, Mexico City? I don't know. Suddenly I have to leave right now" (YL, p. 46).[11]

"In Search of Yage" also introduces new subjects and techniques, which are later incorporated into *Naked Lunch*. New materials include the visions produced by yage, especially the composite city and the blue wave; the imagery of dilapidated South American cities, their corrupt citizens, and the expatriate community; the image of the South American street boy as a physical ideal; the combined political and religious control of human beings by the worst scoundrels on every level of civilization from the primitive jungle tribes to modern urban society; irrational and oppressive police tactics; and tropical diseases and cancer as a metaphor for evil.

New techniques are the expansion of the Lee persona, the increased literalism of the form, and the introduction of the "routine." The persona acquires some new characteristics in addition to that of the objective observer: Lee becomes more humorous, his language more colloquial, and he assumes more and more the pose of a storytelling hustler—a denizen of the underworld he describes. While the persona becomes more fictionalized, the form of the narrative pretends to be strictly factual—a seemingly unrevised series of letters written during the excursion. The expansion of the persona is accompanied by a new kind of narrative episode, which Burroughs calls a "routine": a satirical fantasy improvised from a factual base. In the 23 May note Burroughs says the routine came to him in a dream from which he woke up laughing, indicating that a routine has its source in the irrational world of dreams and is, therefore, a kind of "vision." The laughter implies release and pleasure no matter how negative the subject or how vicious the satire.

The routine mentioned in the 23 May letter, identified in a footnote as "Roosevelt After Inauguration," was not printed in *The Yage Letters*. This satire on Roosevelt's political ploys after taking office was first published in *Floating Bear,* no. 9, in 1961, and seized by the Post Office for obscenity. This routine has since been reprinted many times. The footnote to the letter, probably written by Ginsberg, states that this is Burroughs's first routine. In fact, however, the earlier story of Billy Bradshinkel in the letter of 15 January is also a routine based on a memory of adolescence. It is immediately followed by two short routines, one a fantasy and one a memory. Furthermore, "Twilight's Last Gleaming," written by Burroughs with Kells Elvins in 1938 and later published in *Nova Express* in 1964, is also a routine, showing that Burroughs had developed this form very early, even before seriously beginning a career as a writer. But the letter in "In Search of Yage" is the first time Burroughs refers to the routine form, showing that he is consciously developing routines as part of his repertoire. His notes from this point on were to include many routines that eventually found their way into *Naked Lunch, The Soft Machine, The Ticket That Exploded,* and *Nova Express*.

The Apomorphine Cure

At the end of 1953 Burroughs settled in Tangier, where morphine was easy to obtain and where other artists and writers had found an inexpensive and tolerant environment. From 1953 to 1959 Burroughs published no new fiction, but he continued to accumulate notes and routines. The final stages of his addiction and the success of Dr. Dent's apomorphine treatment in 1957 provided important material for his subsequent novels.[12] Two essays and part 4 of *The Job* show how Burroughs transforms these autobiographical events into fiction.

Burroughs describes himself in the state of "terminal addiction" and his cure through the apomorphine treatment in two important essays: "Deposition: Testimony Concerning a Sickness,"[13] and "Kicking Drugs: A Very Personal Story."[14] These two essays develop further Burroughs's pseudoscience of addiction, incorporating the apomorphine cure into a total construct that is really metaphorical and poetic rather than theoretical and scientific. Burroughs always insists that addiction is a physical, not a psychological, disease. Any person exposed to the experience of opiates is liable to become an addict, regardless of his psychological makeup. Because the euphoria produced by opiates is extremely pleasurable, most human beings want to repeat it over and over again. Once an addict, the person becomes psychologically the same as other addicts; it is as if the addict has been taken over by another personality. Apomorphine, "like a policeman," evicts the addict personality from the host's body without taking over itself: "It does its work and goes."[15] For Burroughs, apomorphine is a liberator, freeing the former addict from his body, which has become externalized and alien through the dynamics of addiction. In the novels written after his cure, apomorphine is used as a metaphor for individual freedom.

In part 4 of *The Job*, "Academy 23," Burroughs discusses the role of drugs and the apomorphine treatment in both his life and art. The discussion of autobiographical fact is interspersed with Burroughs's pseudoscientific theories of addiction, his analysis of the United States government's policies on drugs, and fictional fantasies on the theme of addiction. Some passages in this section were previously published in "Deposition," "Kicking Drugs," and the Academy Series, which had appeared in the British journal *Mayfair* from 1967 to 1969. *The Job* actually shows Burroughs in the process of weaving together fact and fiction. He discusses his own personal experience within the context of his theory of exposure. His experience of Dr. Dent's cure and Dent's own analysis of apomorphine are linked to his metaphorical idea of apomorphine as a "good policeman." The rejection of the apomorphine treatment by the Federal Narcotics Department, the American Medical Association, and the press is attributed to a conspiracy to spread the narcotics problem in the United States in order to expand bureaucratic control, especially to control youth. The present state of affairs is contrasted with Burroughs's fictional academy for youth, which teaches individual autonomy. In Burroughs's imaginary academy cadets are taught preventive health and preventive crime, with apomorphine as the metaphorical model for the proper regulation of the individual and his society. Burroughs told Odier that apomorphine literally saved his life and made his art possible,[16] and in the fictional episodes in *The Job* he transforms this event into a central metaphor.

The Publication of *Naked Lunch*

From 1957 to 1959 Burroughs worked on putting together the manuscript of *Naked Lunch,* which meant selecting and editing from a thousand pages of notes. The task must have been a difficult one, and it is during this period that Burroughs decided on the final form the novel would take. Again, he has emphasized the help and encouragement of others in preparing the manuscript: Kerouac and Ginsberg helped in Tangier in 1957, Gysin and Sinclair Beiles of Olympia Press assisted in Paris in 1959, and Ginsberg later acted as intermediary with Grove Press, the American publisher.

Aside from the problem of editing the manuscript, another reason for Burroughs's delay in publication was the difficulty of finding a sympathetic publisher and the threat of censorship. Once Maurice Girodias of Olympia Press had published *Naked Lunch* in France, Grove Press began preparations for publication in the United States, well aware of possible legal difficulties. *Lady Chatterley's Lover, Howl,* and *Tropic of Cancer* were subjected to censorship trials at that time, and United States Customs was confiscating copies of *Naked Lunch* brought into the country from France. In 1959 University of Chicago officials had prohibited publication of excerpts from *Naked Lunch* in the *Chicago Review*. When the editors resigned and formed an independent journal called *Big Table* in order to publish Burroughs, the first issue was seized by the Post Office because of the material from *Naked Lunch*. In 1961 *Floating Bear* was confiscated by postal authorities because it contained a Burroughs routine, "Roosevelt After Inauguration."

After Grove published *Naked Lunch* in 1962, the publisher defended the novel in a censorship trial in Boston and prepared to defend the book in Los Angeles as well. The case in Los Angeles was dismissed at a hearing in 1965. The judge at the Boston trial in 1965 declared *Naked Lunch* to be obscene. The case was appealed to the Massachusetts Supreme Court, which reversed the decision in 1966. The Boston trial of *Naked Lunch* is significant because it is the last major censorship trial of a work of literature in the United States and because of the noted writers and critics who testified for the defense, including Norman Mailer, Allen Ginsberg, John Ciardi, and Norman Holland. As Michael Barry Goodman remarks in his book on the subject, "*Naked Lunch* has earned its unique distinction as the last work of literature to be censored by the academy, the U.S. Post Office, the U.S. Customs Service, and state and local government."[17]

The Massachusetts Supreme Court finally declared that *Naked Lunch* was not obscene based on criteria that had been established by the United States Supreme Court in a series of cases in the 1950s and 1960s.[18] The most significant Supreme Court cases during this period were *Roth* v. *The United States* (1957) and *Memoirs* v. *Massachusetts* (1966). The *Roth* case established the "social-value test" as the main test of obscenity; that is, a publication could not be judged obscene if it contained ideas having social importance. In the *Memoirs* case, the Court stated that, for a work to be judged obscene, three elements must coalesce: (1) the dominant theme of the material taken as a whole appeals to the prurient interest, (2) the material is patently offensive because it affronts community standards, and (3) the material is "utterly without redeeming social value." Based on these criteria, the Massachusetts Supreme Court found that *Naked Lunch* was not without social value and, therefore, not obscene. The opinion of the literary community and the fact that advertisements for the book did not exploit prurient appeal were also important factors in the decision.[19]

Naked Lunch was the last literary work to be subjected to a major censorship trial in the United States and marked the end of an era that began in the 1870s when the crusader Anthony Comstock persuaded federal and state governments to create and enforce stricter obscenity laws. Since 1966 legal authorities have avoided prosecution of literary works and printed matter in general, although not of other media (i.e., films, pictures, live performances). Although the 1973 Supreme Court decision *Miller* v. *California* revised the strict *Memoirs* criteria and gave local communities more leeway, this legal precedent has not resulted in a change in attitude toward literature. Thus the *Naked Lunch* trial was the final step in eliminating censorship of the printed word in the United States today.

The New Vision of *Naked Lunch*

Naked Lunch purports to be a record of a man's addiction to opiates, his apomorphine treatment, and cure. On the literal level the novel can be seen as the disjointed memories and hallucinations of withdrawal. The "Introduction" and the "Atrophied Preface" (last section) frame the novel in these terms and instruct the reader in how to read the book. The untitled first section recapitulates the action of *Junkie* and ends with the narrator in Tangier. The style of this section shows a further development of the experimentation in "In Search of Yage," Lee, the narrator-protagonist, has assumed totally the addict-hustler personality, and the narrative is interspersed with satirical fantasy episodes. In the second section ("Benway") and throughout the rest of the book, fantasy takes over, transforming Tangier into the imaginary realm of Interzone, and the experience of addiction and withdrawal is used as a basis for social satire.

Naked Lunch represents the same quest through drugs found in *Junkie* and "In Search of Yage" but without hope of transcendence. In *Naked Lunch* the quest finally ends in heightened visions of the here and now. Again and again the novel explodes into visionary episodes that reveal the permanent alienation of the disillusioned protagonist who opposes the delusions of addiction with his new insight: "*I Don't Want To Hear Any More Tired Old Junk Talk and Junk Con. . . .* The same things said a million times and more and there is no point in saying anything because *NOTHING Ever Happens* in the junk world" (NL, p. xiii).[20] The introduction rejects the earlier endless quest for nirvana as self-deceptive and suicidal escapism. All drugs have been tried and all have led to greater bondage rather than freedom from the conditions of physical and social existence.

The terms "addiction" and "junk" are not to be interpreted only on the literal level in *Naked Lunch*; they are also metaphors for the human condition. From the former addict's special angle of vision he perceives that all of humanity is victimized by some form of addiction. The addict's experience has led to the realization that the body is a biological trap and society is run by "control addicts" who use the needs of the body to satisfy their obsession with power. Thus the narrator can say: *"The junk virus is public health problem number one of the world today"* (NL, p. xii).

In *Naked Lunch* Burroughs is conveying a message that is metaphorically stated and visionary in intensity, not simply reporting observations as in *Junkie.* His subject is a state of mind, not a quest. The action is the flow of consciousness, not the travels of a geographical wanderer. But because he is working in a narrative form, he needs characters, action, and setting to convey his ideas and as a vehicle for satire. The answer to these needs in *Naked Lunch* is the creation of an entire metaphorical world, or a mythology. Drawing upon the popular materials he had explored in earlier fiction, Burroughs begins to build a mythology and to transform himself into a pop artist.

The hustling, amoral life-style of the "carny world" of addicts, criminals, and sexual deviants provides the physical, social, and economic environment of *Naked Lunch.* The chief setting is Interzone, an imaginary dystopia described as the "Composite City." It is a composite of all the places that were the scenes of Burroughs's drug quest: the southern United States, South America, Tangier, and the junk neighborhoods the world over as described in *Junkie.* The name "Interzone" recalls the Canal Zone of Panama, which "In Search of Yage" described as a city of cheap hustlers, sleazy sex, and petty officials: "The Panamanians are about the crummiest people in the Hemisphere" (YL, p. 9). Interzone also refers to Tangier, which was an international zone governed until 1956 by a group of European powers called the Board of Control. The natives are mostly Arabs and South Americans, the southern redneck County Clerk governs the town on the frontier, and the colonized Island opposite the Zone is a parody of Gibraltar. The settings are reminiscent of the shifting, amorphous, and decaying junk neighborhoods of *Junkie.* Interzone is the modern city as Waste Land, in which all the cities, peoples, and governments of the world are combined into one huge beehive of commerce, sex, addiction, political manipulation, and rivalry.

Interzone is also described as a single building consisting of bedrooms and a polyglot Market "where all human potentials are spread out" (NL, p. 106). Inhabitants spend their time copulating, shooting up, and making deals in a parody of Western capitalist-consumer societies. Sexuality is on the level of pornography, particularly the "blue movie"; all inhabitants are addicted to drugs, sex, or power; and all commerce is on the level of vice and confidence tricks. The economic theories of capitalism's apologists or its Marxist critics are replaced by Burroughs's Algebra of Need, outlined in the introduction. Pyramids of power and wealth are built from man's total need for drugs, sex, or power, and junk traffic supplies the model for all economic and political empires: "Junk is the ideal product . . . the ultimate merchandise. No sales talk necessary. The client will crawl through a sewer and beg to buy. . . . The junk merchant does not sell his product to the consumer, he sells the consumer to the product. He does not improve and simplify his merchandise. He degrades and simplifies his client. He pays his staff in junk" (NL, p. vii).

Burroughs's political analysis is a form of the conspiracy theory, the common man's perennial answer to the problems of history and government. A secret few conspire to manipulate and control the many. The political parties of Interzone seek to rule the world through total physical and mental control of the human race; they are all "control addicts" who oppose individualism and nonconformity. Religious leaders are given short shrift as part of the power elite that manipulates the masses. One short section on religion reduces the great religions of the world and their founders to "The Prophet Hour," the religion of radio and TV preachers and revivalists' tents, that is, religion as carnival entertainment. The basic carny social relationship of conman and mark, controller and victim, is the basis of Burroughs's pop analysis of power and the social order.

The science and art of this world are also drawn from popular culture. The science of *Naked Lunch* is the popularized scientific knowledge of the mass media (obsessed as Burroughs is with the causes and cures of cancers and viruses) and the pseudoscience of Hubbard's Scientology, Wilhelm Reich's orgonomy, and Burroughs's analysis of addiction and the apomorphine cure. For Burroughs these systems of thought can, like popular art, reveal what is suppressed by currently accepted theories: "Well, these nonconventional theories frequently touch on something going on that Harvard and M.I.T. can't explain. I don't mean that I endorse them wholeheartedly, but I am interested in any attempt along those lines."[21] Furthermore, a pseudoscience tries to give an all-inclusive formula for natural phenomena, which conventional science has never attained, usually communicated through a metaphorical system of ideas, that is, a mythology. A pseudoscientific panacea appeals to the popular mind; the mythological form suits Burroughs's style of thinking and creating.

Naked Lunch begins to develop the pop mythology that the later works elaborate and complete. In *Naked Lunch* Burroughs transforms the body's addictive nature into an entity called the "Human Virus" or the "evil virus." The virus lives upon the human host, satisfying its own needs for

drugs, sex, or power (the three basic addictions for Burroughs) through
demonic possession, which dehumanizes the human being by making him
subservient to a physical or psychological need. When addicted/possessed,
the human being becomes identical with the virus and regresses to a lower
form of life. Numerous transformations in the novel from man to subhuman organism illustrate this hypothesis. Willie the Disk, for example, is
an informer-addict whom police use as a bloodhound. Bradley the Buyer
is addicted to contact with junkies and becomes a man-eating monster
eventually destroyed by flame throwers. Dr. Schafer's "de-anxietized man"
turns into a giant black centipede. The most important episode illustrating this process is the story of "the talking asshole" told by Benway in the
central section of the book: "Ordinary Men and Women." In this story, a
man is taken over by one of his bodily functions (the "lowest") and reduced
to "one all-purpose blob." The episode is brilliantly funny and terrifying
at the same time. At the end of the story, Benway points out the moral
and puts forth Burroughs's own views about "the basic American rottenness" revealed by popular culture, and the dangers of bureaucracies, which
are like cancers or viruses (NL, pp. 133–34).

In Burroughs's mythology, the social structure mirrors the individual
process of addiction/possession on a larger scale. The social dynamic of addiction is that of predator and victim, the Algebra of Need: "The face of
'evil' is always the face of total need. . . . In the words of total need:
'*Wouldn't you?*' Yes you would. You would lie, cheat, inform on your
friends, steal, do *anything* to satisfy total need. Because you would be in a
state of total sickness, total possession, and not in a position to act in any
other way" (NL, p. vii). The major social institutions built upon this can-
nibalistic structure are also viruses or cancers (cancer is said to be a virus in
Naked Lunch), which take over the healthy social body and warp it to fill
the needs of a parasitic organism, eventually leading the human race to
destruction. The Narcotic Bureau, for example, is cited as a parasitic social
agency seeking to perpetuate itself through increasing its scope and powers. The orgasm-death of the hanged man, a recurrent image, also illustrates the evil of the social system based on the Algebra of Need. The
imagery of downward metamorphosis and the orgasm of the hanged man,
which previously appeared in *Junkie*, assume an even greater importance in
Naked Lunch as repeated motifs illustrating the mythology of addiction.

As in *Junkie*, the most important characters representing social controllers are doctors. Politicians and religious leaders receive far less attention
because doctors' central role in a mythology of addiction corresponds to
what Burroughs sees as their central role in American society: those who
use science and technology to control and degrade man. And in the popu-

lar mind, doctors are the most highly respected professionals in the United States. Dr. Benway, Dr. Fingers Schafer ("The Lobotomy Kid"), Dr. Berger, and the German doctor of "Joselito" represent the type of the mad scientist and parody the modern scientist's disregard for the human and social results of his experimentation. Benway is the servant of repressive social systems, using his knowledge to control human behavior. The end of his experiments is the IND (Irreversible Neural Damage), a body without a mind. Dr. Schafer produces the "Complete All American De-Anxietized Man," a black centipede. Dr. Berger creates perfectly healthy men through brainwashing that removes all thought. When his "overliberated" end-products lose their usefulness as subjects, they are sent to "disposal." These controllers who use knowledge and power to dehumanize complement the subhuman victims that appear elsewhere in the novel. Both types are derived from the caricatures in *Junkie,* but the mythic context of *Naked Lunch* gives these types greater artistic power.

The action of the myth consists of a battle between the forces of good and evil for control of the human individual and the human race. The three conspiratorial parties of Interzone—the Liquefactionists, the Divisionists, and the Senders—seek to rule the world through parasitic possession. They are all "control addicts." All three parties attempt to make all men conform to a single image reflecting the person or force in control. The Liquefactionists, the party of the far right, plan to liquidate everyone but themselves. Carried to its logical conclusion, liquidation would ultimately eliminate everyone except one man. This party is a parody of modern totalitarianism and racism. Sexually, it is associated with sadomasochism. The Divisionists, the moderate party, plan to take over by flooding the world with their own replicas, or clones. Again, the goal is domination by one man (and one sex) through eliminating everyone except one set of replicas. This party is a parody of the biblical creation of man, homosexuality, and the conspiracy theory of politics.

The totalitarian party of the left is the Senders, whose members attempt to control everyone through mental telepathy, the greatest evil of all according to Burroughs. Again, Sending must lead to only one man in control of a brainwashed subhuman population. The ultimate Sender or villain of the myth is Salvador Hassan O'Leary, who plays all the villainous roles in the novel under various aliases. Senders are associated with addiction, the totalitarian Mayan civilization, the downward metamorphosis of man to insect, and the use of science for evil purposes—some of Burroughs's major themes. In fact, the Senders are identified as the ultimate enemy, and Sending seems to underlie all the evils of control. Sending is called an addiction (NL, p. 168), a cancer (NL, p. 155), and is finally identified as the Human Virus (NL, p. 168).

The only force fighting these evil parasites is the Factualist party, the fourth party of Interzone. The Factualists are a radical group that represents anarchic individualism, as Eric Mottram first pointed out.[22] Factualist agents attempt to foil the plots of the villains simply by revealing them. In a way, the entire novel can be seen as such a revelation, and the two Factualists in the book—Lee the Agent and A. J.—are Burroughs's alter egos. Factualist revelation is equated with the murder of a villain and with the apomorphine cure for addiction. There is a flaw in the Factualist program, however. Since all the agents are human, they are all potential addicts who may succumb at any moment: "all Agents defect and all Resisters sell out" (NL, p. 205). Thus the situation is never resolved; the cosmic battle between good and evil goes on and on, like the continuing plot of a comic-strip adventure, as Burroughs remarked in an interview with Ann Morrisette.[23]

Salvador Hassan O'Leary and A. J., mortal enemies representing the controllers and the liberators, are very much alike as characters in that neither has any permanent personality or identity and both assume many similar roles. This is shown most clearly in two sections, "Hassan's Rumpus Room" and "A. J.'s Annual Party," in which each character sponsors a similar sex orgy. Only the results of their actions reveal that Hassan uses tricks to profit and control, and A. J. uses jokes to expose and liberate. Hassan and A. J. are not characters, but opposing forces that assume many shapes. In *Junkie* Burroughs began to portray characters as the locus of impersonal forces; in the mythic world of *Naked Lunch,* this kind of character is the vehicle for the godlike powers of a Manichaean universe.

Bill Lee, Burroughs's version of himself as addict-writer, is another "character" who barely exists except for his voice and his actions. The persona is even more of a cipher than before, appearing at the beginning and end as the withdrawing addict and Factualist Agent. Lee's voice is that of the hipster-addict, telling stories about his adventures. He has the tone and vocabulary of the carnival barker, the street hustler, or the conman. Lee's actions are those of the Factualist Agent: he infiltrates enemy organizations, reveals their plots, and thereby "murders" evil. His unpunished murder of Officers Hauser and O'Brien in the last episode is a metaphor for factualist liberation. Because the police are seeking to confiscate his manuscripts as well as his drugs, his gun, and his person, Agent Lee is also the writer of *Naked Lunch,* who destroys evil by writing about it.

The title "naked lunch" refers to the authorial intention to "reveal the facts." The "naked lunch" means both the act of seeing and what is seen. Use of the title in the introduction and the preface establishes the naked lunch as seeing, and particularly seeing the naked lunch itself "on the end of every fork" or "on the end of that long newspaper spoon." Within the body of the book, the naked lunch of human life is portrayed as cannibalism, oral-anal sex, orgasm-death, and coprophagy. "To lunch" is to see the vision but also to be a part of it, for no one can escape the human condition. Only a kind of mental freedom is implied by the act of seeing clearly.

In using pseudoscience to create a popular mythology, Burroughs is entering the realm of popular literature: popular science becomes science fiction. In *Naked Lunch* Burroughs makes use of the full range of popular literary resouces: news media, advertising, and popular fiction in all of its forms (magazines, paperbacks, comics, movies, radio, and television serials). From all of these and from his own contact with the underworld, Burroughs gains his enviable command of popular speech—vocabulary, idioms, and rhythms. From news media and advertising, Burroughs also adopts the goal of writing to change consciousness: "*Naked Lunch* is a blueprint, a How-To Book . . . How-To extend levels of experience" (NL, p. 224).

From the various forms of popular fiction, Burroughs derives his plot, characters, and many characteristic images. *Naked Lunch* draws from the detective story, the gothic tale, older science fiction of the mad-doctor variety, and pornography. The popular motifs from these fictions include the secret agent, the alienated private eye, the mobster boss and his gang, the mad doctor and amoral scientific experimenter, monsters, zombies, vampires, body snatchers, space-time travel, secret plots, secret formulas or weapons, intelligent nonhuman beings, nearly inhuman villains, sadomasochistic fantasies, and other perversions. What all these popular forms have in common is a paranoid view of the world that Burroughs accepts as valid. Popular art, like pseudoscience, reveals what society would like to repress. As Benway remarks at one point in the novel, "there's always a space *between,* in popular songs and Grade B movies, giving away the basic American rottenness" (NL, p. 133).

The New Form of *Naked Lunch*

The new vision of *Naked Lunch* is presented in an experimental form derived from painting, photography, film, and jazz. The basic technique Burroughs chose to use is juxtaposition, called collage or montage in the visual arts. The overall structure of *Naked Lunch* is a montage of "routines" that—theoretically—can be read in any order. Burroughs announces this structure in the "Atrophied Preface" when he says, "You can cut into *Naked Lunch* at any intersection point" (NL, p. 224) and "The Word is divided into units which be all in one piece and should be so taken, but the pieces can be had in any order" (NL, p. 229).

Each routine is an independent piece introduced by a title indicating subject or theme. (The first routine is the only one without a caption.) The routines are dramatically realized fantasies consisting of monologues, dialogues, plot episodes, scene descriptions, and collage passages of associative imagery. Within the routines, Burroughs's technique is jazzlike improvisation. Typically, Burroughs begins with a person, a conversation, or an event that is factual or credible and improvises on this theme in a fantastic and satiric vein. The routines in *Naked Lunch* vary in length from two or three pages to twenty-five pages. The shorter ones consist of one or two episodes; the longer ones contain several. Structure within routines is based on a rhythm of expansion and contraction: statement of theme, improvisation, climax, sometimes return to theme, and then a new improvisation. Narrative transitions may be provided (such as a character in one scene introducing a story) or episodes may be juxtaposed without transition. As improvisational flights continue, Burroughs often carries a narrative through to a violent, chaotic conclusion with an "all hell breaking loose" effect. The riots at the end of the "Benway" and "Ordinary Men and Women" sections are examples of building up to an explosive climax. Sometimes improvisation leads to a collage passage: a prose poem of juxtaposed images built around a single theme. The end of "Algebra of Need," "Hauser and O'Brien," and the "Quick" section, which concludes the "Atrophied Preface," are examples. These collage passages are static and descriptive. The effect is contemplative rather than violent.

The work as a whole exhibits this organic and improvisational pattern. *Naked Lunch* begins with the factual and autobiographical introduction, which explains the author's addiction and cure, and the first routine, which recapitulates the biographical journey of *Junkie*. From this base, the novel moves into fantasies of addiction and control, building up to the central routines: "The Market," "Ordinary Men and Women," "Islam Incorporated and the Parties of Interzone," "The County Clerk," and "Interzone." This group of routines in the heart of the book contains the most detailed, concentrated descriptions of Interzone, its inhabitants, and the mythic plot, as well as Burroughs's most wide-ranging social satire. The remaining routines return primarily to the themes of addiction and control, but with the added themes of escape and rebellion. The later routines also include more collage sections than those in the first half of the book. *Naked Lunch* ends with an autobiographical preface that discusses quite directly the novel's technique and metaphors and a clinical appendix that lists and discusses drugs mentioned in the novel. Thus the work is framed by factual, autobiographical sections that address the reader directly, guiding him into and out of an extraordinary text. Although the routines can stand alone and the form is a montage, the order is not random. There is an overall psychological pattern, an order of increasing complexity in the use of experimental technique, and a didactic frame.

Burroughs chose a montage and improvisational structure for *Naked Lunch* for three reasons: it is a way to present the flow of consciousness; it is a way to expand the reader's consciousness, and it is an effective satirical technique. *Naked Lunch* is overtly presented as a record of the writer's consciousness: "There is only one thing a writer can write about: *what is in front of his senses at the moment of writing.* . . . I am a recording instrument. . . . I do not presume to impose 'story' 'plot' 'continuity.' . . . Insofar as I succeed in *Direct* recording of certain areas of psychic process I may have a limited function. . . . I am not an entertainer . . ." (NL, p. 221). Thus the mythic content is autobiograhical; the characters are Burroughs's alter egos; the plot, his inner conflicts; the structure, that of his actual experience; the texture, that of his individual perceptions; the themes, his own spiritual quest and discovery. The unusual composition is explained as Burroughs's stream of consciousness and as a random collection of notes. Furthermore, the introduction and preface state that the novel consists of notes taken during the withdrawal sickness of a drug cure— a paranoid schizophrenic state that gives the surreal visions the status of fact. Withdrawal also produces uncontrollable sociability and the revelation of distasteful intimacies, according to *Junkie*. *Naked Lunch* is even more literal as unmediated experience than the confessional *Junkie* and the epistolary "In Search of Yage": it is a diary that records experience as it happens, and the act of recording is part of the experience.

The effect of montage, however, is a new vision. Juxtaposition asks the reader to make connections between the elements that are set next to each other. The new mental associations are a form of expanded consciousness. Furthermore, the lack of conventional literary narrative gives powerful impact to the images presented, which are taken out of their ordinary context and assume a dreamlike power. Thus *Naked Lunch* is presented as "revelation and prophecy" (NL, p. 229). It is not only a record of one individual's vision, but an attempt to re-create that vision in the reader.

Both juxtaposition and improvisational fantasy fulfill a satirical function in *Naked Lunch*. These techniques enable Burroughs to use his popular materials as a weapon for attacking the social order. Montage juxtaposes the bourgeois and the hipster-addict, public politics and the underworld, legitimate and illegitimate business, organized religion and show business, literary and popular art, science and pseudoscience in order to show the evil inherent in the entire system: the cynical control of the masses of common men by and for the few through basic human physical and psychological needs. The combination of avant-garde technique and critical intention with popular materials is what makes Burroughs a pop artist, not just one who uses popular materials. His literary work is analogous to pop art of the same period.[24]

Extensive use of montage increases the disorder of a composition, but Burroughs has counteracted the centrifugal tendency of montage with several unifying and ordering techniques. One is the order of the routines described above, following a psychological pattern and, to a certain extent, designed to orient and instruct the reader. The mythology also ties the routines together by providing an underlying narrative of which each fragment is a part. Finally, the unifying sensibility of Burroughs lies behind the work: *Naked Lunch* is the creation of one man's consciousness even though he deemphasizes this role by calling himself an "instrument" and by calling attention to the collaboration of others. The vision and the voice of *Naked Lunch* are idiosyncratic, unmistakably the product of one personality called William S. Burroughs.

The Style of *Naked Lunch*

In *Naked Lunch* Burroughs has achieved his mature voice, and the unconventionality of his new style is another element of experimental form in the novel. The style of *Naked Lunch* is oral, colloquial, and parodic. The informal speech of many groups is imitated, particularly the language of the addict underworld. Burroughs has an ear for the vernacular and is extremely successful in presenting the spoken word. His sensitivity and skill are such that the novel's prose often approaches the status of poetry. The representation of the spoken word in print is responsible for Burroughs's unusual use of typography: his abundant capitals, italics, and ellipses. Capitals and italics are used to indicate tone and emphasis, usually ironic, and ellipses indicate pauses. Ellipses are also used to join juxtaposed images and phrases in the collage passages, providing a nonverbal transition. Capitals and italics are also used for headings that introduce routines or sections, taking the place of narrative transitions. The unusual typography emphasizes the unconventionality of the novel, its fragmentary nature, and the colloquial rather than literary style.

Naked Lunch is also a very funny book, and Burroughs's humor is an important part of his style. Mary McCarthy says that Burroughs's humor is "peculiarly American, at once broad and sly," pointing to the country and vaudeville sources.[25] But this contradictory humor is also a result of the montage technique, which juxtaposes the primitive and the sophisticated, combining humor that is gross and simple, such as calling the hogs in a gourmet restaurant, and some that is verbal and intellectual, such as Benway's description of how he achieves total demoralization: "I deplore brutality. . . . It's not efficient." Burroughs's major comic techniques are satiric: the parody of social types and their language, the undercutting of intellectual pretensions with physical grossness, the exaggeration of the actual in satirical fantasy, taking metaphors literally, and the humorous incongruity of arbitrarily juxtaposed images or episodes, another kind of undercutting technique. Burroughs's obscenity is a major element in his humor, as it is often an element in traditional satire. In fact, Burroughs refers in the introduction to Swift's "A Modest Proposal" as the model for some of his obscene episodes. Grotesque and macabre images of sexuality, violence, and death are used to undercut and ridicule, to shock into moral recognition.

But in spite of all of the parallels with traditional satire, *Naked Lunch* is ultimately a parodic rather than a satiric work. It attacks without implying any positive standard as traditional satire does. The individual, anarchic freedom that lies behind the destructive satire exists in a vacuum, with no moral or social structure to support it or to give satire any function but destruction. The only values upheld by Burroughs's parodic style are the energy, delight, and laughter that come from the freedom from controlling structures and the joy in spontaneous response to inner impulses and external context. These are the hipster's values, and *Naked Lunch* is a Beat masterpiece, embodying the hipster mentality, which Burroughs had explored in life and in *Junkie*.

The Impact of *Naked Lunch*

Naked Lunch has given its author a permanent place in literary history because of its formal innovations, its powerful attitude of revolt, and the controversy surrounding its publication. The censorship trials, of course, attracted publicity, but also attracted the attention of serious readers because of the authors and critics who testified on behalf of the novel. Critical attention was further drawn to *Naked Lunch* when Mary McCarthy and Norman Mailer praised the book highly at the Edinburgh International Writer's Conference in 1962. Mailer proclaimed Burroughs "the only American novelist living today who may conceivably be possessed by genius."[26] Mary McCarthy defended her statement at the conference with an influential essay on *Naked Lunch,* first published in 1963 and still the best single critical piece on Burroughs.[27] Grove Press was able to obtain testimonials for *Naked Lunch* by Mailer, Robert Lowell, Terry Southern, and John Ciardi, among others, for a publicity pamphlet in 1962.

As a result of the high praise by well-known literary figures, *Naked Lunch* was widely reviewed in the United States and England. Many reviewers praised the book for its power and serious purpose, and Burroughs was compared to other avant-garde writers in the modernist tradition. But *Naked Lunch* received strongly negative reviews as well. Some reviewers thought the novel morally offensive, artistically worthless, and revolting to the sensibilities of most readers. The most notable of these protests, because of the correspondence they generated, are those of John Wain in the *New Republic,* William Phillips in *Commentary,* and an unsigned review entitled "Ugh" in the *Times Literary Supplement.*[28] The debate following the *TLS* review was the longest and liveliest in that publication's history. The critical controversy, however, has established *Naked Lunch* as a seminal postwar work that must be continually read and reevaluated regardless of the personal tastes of individual critics.

Chapter Three

A Mythology for the Space Age

In the writing of *Naked Lunch,* Burroughs discovered the style that best conveyed his vision, and its publication released a great deal of creative energy. In quick succession thereafter, Burroughs produced three important novels: *The Soft Machine, The Ticket That Exploded,* and *Nova Express* (published in 1961, 1962, and 1964, respectively).[1] All three of these works were drawn from the same mass of notes that was the source of *Naked Lunch,*[2] and they continue to develop the themes and techniques of that seminal book.

But although the three subsequent novels grow out of *Naked Lunch,* the latter stands alone as a self-contained work while *The Soft Machine, The Ticket That Exploded,* and *Nova Express* form a closely knit, continuously evolving trilogy.[3] Both technique and content separate the trilogy from *Naked Lunch* and bind the three subsequent novels together. The trilogy introduces the radical experimental technique of the cutup and can be seen as an exhaustive exploration of that method of creating nonnarrative prose fiction. The trilogy also makes use of a more comprehensive mythology that is consistently developed throughout all three novels.

All of Burroughs's novels from *Junkie* to *Nova Express* constitute a major series of novels based on his experience as an addict. These works tell the story of an artistic career that combined a dangerous personal quest through drugs and a radical experimentation with the forms of fiction. With the completion of the trilogy, Burroughs had exhausted this particular path of exploration and decided to turn in a new direction as a writer. The trilogy, then, is the artistic culmination of Burroughs's early literary career and, taken as a whole, is a significant achievement. The entire series of works from *Junkie* to *Nova Express* permanently establishes Burroughs as an important postwar American novelist.

The Cutup Technique

Burroughs discovered the cutup in 1959 in Paris through his friend Brion Gysin, a painter. When Gysin began experimenting with cutups in

48

his own work, Burroughs immediately saw the similarity to the juxtaposition technique he had used in *Naked Lunch* and began extensive experiments with text, often with the collaboration of other writers. (Although Burroughs has credited Gysin with discovering the cutup, he has also acknowledged similar literary experiments in the works of Tzara, Stein, Eliot, and Dos Passos.) In 1960 Burroughs published his initial cutup experiments in Paris in *Minutes To Go* (with Brion Gysin, Sinclair Beiles, and Gregory Corso) and in San Francisco in *The Exterminator* (with Brion Gysin), works that were partially intended to introduce the technique to the public. Throughout the 1960s Burroughs and Gysin collaborated on cutup experiments in many media, the most significant collaborations being three films done in 1965 with English filmmaker Antony Balch (*Towers Open Fire, Cut-Ups,* and *Bill and Tony*) and *The Third Mind,* a book first completed in 1965 but not published in English until 1978. The final version of *The Third Mind* is both a historical collection of cutup experiments from 1960 to 1978 and a manifesto that sums up the cutup's significance for Burroughs and Gysin.

The cutup is a mechanical method of juxtaposition in which Burroughs literally cuts up passages of prose by himself and other writers and then pastes them back together *at random*. This literary version of the collage technique is also supplemented by literary use of other media. Burroughs transcribes taped cutups (several tapes spliced into each other), film cutups (montage), and mixed media experiments (results of combining tapes with television, movies, or actual events). Thus Burroughs's use of cutups develops his juxtaposition technique to its logical conclusion as an experimental prose method, and he also makes use of all contemporary media, expanding his use of popular culture.

As Burroughs experimented with the technique, he began to develop a theory of the cutup, and this theory was incorporated into his pseudoscience of addiction. In addition to drugs, sex, and power as aspects of man's addictive nature, Burroughs adds an analysis of control over human beings exercised by language ("the Word"), time, and space (i.e., man's physical existence and the mental constructs he uses to survive and adapt). Drugs, sex, and power control the body, but "word and image locks" control the mind, that is, "lock" us into conventional patterns of perceiving, thinking, and speaking that determine our interactions with environment and society. The cutup is a way of exposing word and image controls and thus freeing oneself from them, an alteration of consciousness that occurs in both the writer and the reader of the text. For Burroughs as an artist, the cutup is an impersonal method of inspiration, invention, and an arrangement that redefines the work of art as a process that occurs in collaboration with others and is not the sole property of artists. Thus Burroughs's cutup texts are comparable to similar contemporary experiments in other arts, such as action painting, happenings, and aleatory music. His theory of the cutup also parallels avant-garde literary theory, such as structuralism and deconstruction.[4]

Burroughs's trilogy is based on the cutup and the theory of language and art that the cutup produced. Through the direct incorporation of cutup material, Burroughs also introduces into the trilogy important new material from popular science and popular literature: the Nova Mob, Nova Police and their training, Reich's orgone accumulators, Scientology's E-meter, sense withdrawal tanks, infrasound, reality as a film, popular evolutionary theories, more use of space/time travel motifs, the spy novel of international conspiracies, the idealized past of the western, and Burroughs's analysis of Mayan civilization and Hassan i Sabbah's legendary assassins. The most important addition from popular culture is the science-fiction material, which Burroughs finds most appropriate to express his analysis of word and image controls and their destruction by the cutup technique. Cutup is equated with space/time, travel, silence, and freedom from the body. Burroughs also incorporates cutups from many literary authors: T. S. Eliot, Kafka, Shakespeare, Conrad, Graham Greene, and Coleridge are the most prominent in the trilogy, and their juxtaposition with banal popular materials is another example of Burroughs's pop-art technique, which integrates high and low culture.

The Nova Mythology

The cutup technique and additional materials from popular culture are combined with Burroughs's montage form to create a "mythology for the space age,"[5] on which the trilogy is based. The plot and characters of this myth provide underlying unity and continuity to a series of novels whose narrative is fragmented. The plot postulates a group of superhuman forces from outer space (the Nova Mob) who control human beings by assuming the form of a parasitic virus. These forces have been in control of the earth for 3,000 years, having come to earth in a space ship after causing the supernova, or star explosion, that produced the Crab Nebula. The Mob has controlled life on earth through the addiction of human beings to word and image, junk, sex, and power. They become viruses, which are two-dimensional, to gain access to the three-dimensional human body through the body's weakness for addiction—pleasure and pain—and infect by making the human a replica of the controller, that is, either an exploiter or victim of word and image, drugs, sex, or power. The goal of the Nova Mob is to produce a Nova on earth as they did in the case of the Crab Nebula.

The Nova Mob is led by Mr. and Mrs. D, alias Mr. Bradly Mr. Martin, alias the Ugly Spirit, who is the controller of word and image (hence the double name). Some members of the Mob, known as Venusians, operate through sexual needs. They are associated with the color green and vegetable life; sexual addiction can reduce men to vegetables or even to primal slime—"green goo." The Venusians are Burroughs's final mythic adaptation of Reich's theory of sexual repression. The criminals who operate through drug addiction are the Uranians, associated with heavy metal, the color blue, coolness, ozone, and a "hifi blue note." In his last metaphorical analysis of addiction, Burroughs says that junk reduces the addict to nonliving material, more metallic than vegetable. The viruses that operate through power addiction are the Crab People, from "the white hot skies of Minraud," somewhere in the Crab Nebula. They are associated with the color white, heat, and ovens, and can turn their addicts into insects. This part of the Mob has evolved from Burroughs's study of Mayan civilization, which he calls the most totalitarian control system known to man, combined with contemporary images of concentration camps and Hiroshima, as well as the behavioristic techniques of mind control taught by Scientology. Thus the popular sciences of Wilhelm Reich, Burroughs and Ron Hubbard merge with the forms of popular science fiction into an original astrology that encompasses the universe and man's place in it. The astrological element adds yet another dimension drawn from popular culture and broadens the scope of the mythic land of Interzone described in *Naked Lunch*.

The Nova Police are not highly individualized. The District Supervisor, technicians, Agent K9, a cadet, and Agent or Inspector Lee are mentioned. The last three, at one time or another, all seem to be alter egos of William S. Burroughs. The Nova Police use technology to combat the Nova criminals. Technology can create apomorphine to regulate addiction and silence to destroy word and image control. Arrests are made by blocking the coordinate points by which the virus invades the human body. Cadets are trained to do this by learning to think and write in association blocks and to avoid being trapped by pleasure, pain, or emotion. Nova Police are associated with silver flashes, flakes, the color gray, panpipes, melting, fading, and wind. These images are also associated with the destruction of word and image and the invasion of silence—what the Nova Police are supposed to accomplish.

The mythology in the trilogy is not superimposed in a mechanical manner, but is an immanent and evolving metaphor within the three novels. The myth is not complete until the end of the trilogy and, in a sense, is never complete because of the open, fragmented nature of Burroughs's fiction. For example, some elements appear only once or in only one of the novels and are never developed further. Repeated elements gain new significance in new contexts but are never fixed in form or meaning. Yet, even though Burroughs's presentation of the mythology is not systematic, thematic emphases give each novel its own subjects and limits. The *Soft Machine* focuses primarily on the historical control of mankind through bodily needs. *The Ticket That Exploded* focuses on the present and on control of the mind through word and image. *Nova Express* predicts a future apocalypse and recapitulates the entire mythology. Thus the trilogy encompasses a total cosmology of past, present, and future.

Time Travel in *The Soft Machine*

The Soft Machine consists of seventeen relatively brief chapters, or routines. (Most are fewer than ten pages: the longest is a little over twenty pages.) Each routine contains both improvisational narrative episodes similar in style to the satirical fantasies of *Naked Lunch* and cutup material. The narrative episodes within routines, however, are usually much briefer than those in *Naked Lunch.* The shorter narrative passages in combination with cutup collage passages make up a highly fragmented work in which the juxtaposition technique dominates the consciousness of the reader. The book must be read slowly and carefully, like a poem, and one must focus on imagery, theme, and associative relationships, rather than on chronological-causal structures. Much more than *Naked Lunch,* the effect of *The Soft Machine* is kaleidoscopic, and the order of the routines seems even more arbitrary.

The Soft Machine, however, is not entirely a random collection of fragments. Each routine does have general thematic unity, and each is related to the book's major theme: the social control of mankind throughout human history by the manipulation of bodily needs. The novel's thesis is conveyed in two ways: through image clusters that create thematic emphasis and through specific fantasies that receive emphasis because of narrative coherence and length. As in *Naked Lunch,* sexuality, drugs, and power are the three types of control, but *The Soft Machine* gives different emphasis to these themes and also adds the theme of revolt.

Sexuality as a means of social control is the major theme of *The Soft*

Machine, leading to a predominance of sexual scenes and Burroughs's repertoire of sexual imagery: memories and fantasies of adolescent homosexual and autoerotic experiences, travel South, South American people and places, tropical climate (warmth, humidity, steaminess), plant life (especially jungles, vines, plant juice and slime), primitive and amorphous life forms (jelly, slime, protoplasm, tissue), water (rivers, mud, showers), refuse (mud, sewage, garbage, slime, compost heaps), odors of decomposition, the carnival (penny arcades, Interzone-like carnival cities of sexual activity), the withdrawal orgasm, and the orgasm-death of hanging or other torture. This imagery is drawn from personal experience, popular cultural stereotypes, and literary tradition (in particular, Burroughs includes in cutup form the city and water imagery from *The Waste Land*). Characterization in *The Soft Machine* is so minimal that characters become motifs rather than persons. Characters associated with the sexual theme are drawn from autobiography (memories and personal fantasies), anthropological fantasy (imaginary South American tribes with unusual sexual practices; Carl the traveler), historical fantasy (Johnny Yen—the transsexual Survival Artist of the ages, the Countess de Vile—the decadent jetsetter, ancient priests serving the Corn God and the Earth Mother), the science-fiction Nova mythology (the Venus Mob, the Vegetable People, the Green Boys), and other literature (Danny Deever, Melville's Billy Budd, the hanged god of T. S. Eliot).

Control through drugs receives less emphasis than sexuality, but the imagery of the addict world and the metaphor of addiction are important secondary motifs. *The Soft Machine* includes the familiar imagery of junk neighborhoods, possession by an evil force, downward metamorphosis, versions of the Algebra of Need, and various addict-hustlers (Lee, the Sailor, Johnny, Bill, Bill Gains, Benway, Green Tony). The color blue, heavy metal, the smell of ozone, coldness, and a "blue" note are junk images that link the theme of addiction to the Uranians of the Nova mythology. Finally, the narrator of *The Soft Machine* consistently assumes the persona of the hustler-storyteller of the carny world, whether he plays the role of conman, Nova criminal, or Nova agent. Thus the vision and the voice of the carny world permeate the novel even though drug addiction is not its major subject, and this persona has the same reductive and satirical effect as in *Naked Lunch*.

The theme of power is primarily conveyed through narrative fantasy. *The Soft Machine* contains five relatively sustained fantasies, which, because of their length and coherence as narratives amid so much cutup material, dominate the reader's interpretation of the text. All five of these narratives are dystopian fantasies, each one taking place in a different period of human history. It is these dystopias that give *The Soft Machine* its historical emphasis, and the following analysis will discuss them chronologically although they do not appear in chronological order in the text. In fact, the fantasy that is earliest in time is actually placed at the end of the book.

In "Cross the Wounded Galaxies," the last routine of *The Soft Machine,* Burroughs invents a story of how mankind began: his creation myth. Burroughs imagines the beginning of humanity as a biological disaster story. Apes become human as a result of a virus infection that kills most of the species and mutates the rest. The survivors feel a painful invasion of their bodies by an external force that gradually produces human behavior. Humanity develops from language ("the talk sickness"), eating flesh and excrement (cannibalism is implied), and sexuality. Clearly, this episode portrays the invasion of the Nova Mob on earth, but it is told from the point of view of the ignorant victims, who must adapt to painful mutations as they become "soft machines." The soft machine is the human body controlled by physical needs, which can be manipulated through language. The body itself is not evil, but the psychophysical control mechanisms are, and it is these that make bodily existence a trap. Characteristically, Burroughs's metaphysical view is conveyed in a fiction that draws from pseudoscientific and science-fiction sources. His prose, however, is more poignantly poetic than in any other section of the novel as he describes the dawn of consciousness.

The fantasy of Puerto Joselito in "Pretend an Interest" (ninth routine) is an anthropological fantasy on preliterate societies based on Burroughs's South American travels and his anthropological studies. This fantasy portrays primitive man as wholly enslaved by psychosexual control systems. Puerto Joselito, a carnival-city on the mudflats of a river in the middle of a South American jungle, is described entirely through Burroughs's sexual imagery. The fantastic inhabitants are always engaged in sadistic sexual activity, and many have the form of sex organs. The city is ruled by priests of various cults who conduct ritual executions. Orgasm-death is described over and over as the fundamental religious ritual, which is the basis of all religious and political control. The priest-rulers are associated with the power imagery Burroughs uses for his Mayan and Minraud fantasies. Puerto Joselito is Burroughs's reinterpretation of Frazier's *The Golden Bough* and a critique of religion in Reichian terms. It is both an homage to and a reinterpretation of *The Waste Land.*

The theme of power is given its most detailed treatment in "The Mayan Caper," a historical fantasy on Mayan civilization (seventh routine). "The

Mayan Caper" is the single most significant section of *The Soft Machine* because of its central placement in the text, because it is the longest sustained narrative, and because it gives the most straightforward exposition of how a control system works and how it can be dismantled. The Mayans are presented both as the historical beginning and the epitome of "civilization": a social order in which a few control the many through manipulation of word and image. Literacy only makes the control system more sophisticated. The Mayan priest-ruler class controls the mass of peasants through their calendar, a word-and-image system that orders time, space, and human behavior. The calendar is the basis for the Mayans' agricultural economy, their hierarchical system of classes, and their religion. The priests exert total mind control and thus have total mastery over the peasants' bodies. The power imagery associated with the Mayans is the same as that of the Minraud people in the Nova mythology: religious sacrifice, insects, ants, centipedes, scorpions, crabs, lobsters, claws, white heat, and the city. The first part of the "I Sekuin" routine, which immediately follows "The Mayan Caper," makes the link to Minraud explicit and again emphasizes the importance of the Mayan fantasy as the classic type of all control systems.

The Trak fantasy in "Trak Trak Trak" (fourth routine) is a satire on contemporary capitalist-consumer societies. Trak is an international corporation that sells junk–like products producing total dependency on "Trak servicing." Trak advertises and sells products like a corporation, controls unconscious thinking through advertising ("Trak Sex and Dream Utilities"), controls conscious thinking through the news media ("Trak News Agency" specifically refers to the Hearst and Luce empires), and runs a totalitarian state called the Trak Reservation in Freelandt (an allusion to Sweden's welfare state). Trak is a total modern control system based on the economics of junk as described in *Naked Lunch*. Trak is thus linked to the Nova mythology by junk imagery and is associated with the Uranian Mob.

The final important narrative in *The Soft Machine* appears in "Gongs of Violence" (fifteenth routine). Slotless City is a futuristic fantasy of violence and chaos produced by sexual conflict. Through insoluble conflict the Nova Mob seeks to destroy the earth, and the Slotless City fantasy envisions sexual conflict as the cause of a future apocalypse. This narrative portrays science-fiction methods of reproduction in a society in which men and women are at war, leading to the creation of fantastic new life forms fighting with each other for existence, and ending with the destruction of all life on earth. The final apocalypse is conveyed in ambiguous cutup imagery. It is unclear whether the destruction is positive or negative, a victory for the Mob or for the Police, for the disintegration of present reality structures is a form of liberation from control.

Gradually, a thesis emerges from *The Soft Machine*'s thematic focus on sexuality and power within a historical framework. For Burroughs, the history of sexuality *is* the history of power, and his analysis of sexual repression is essentially Reichian.[6] All control systems are based on the repression and manipulation of sexuality for the benefit of a ruling class, and all power structures are essentially the same since they are all built upon biological necessity. Thus for Burroughs, history is a process of repetitions, not a progression: a "penny arcade peep show long process in different forms." As long as "human nature" (or—more accurately—our concept of human nature) remains the same, history is but a series of permutations in which specific forms may change, but not the underlying system of relationships. And, by implication, if history is simply a repetitive series of fixed relationships, the writer can create fictions that are just as true as history. Thus, Burroughs's fictional narratives in *The Soft Machine* are history. Later in the trilogy, Burroughs illustrates the corollary that history is fiction.

Within this thematic context, the image of orgasm-death takes on an expanded meaning. The orgasm-death of the hanged man in *Naked Lunch* was the symbol of a predatory social order based on human need. In *The Soft Machine* it is the symbol of religious power, the moral authority that legitimizes political systems of control. Burroughs points out that the ritual of human sacrifice lies behind every mythology, and that a sadistic god of death authorizes traditional social and economic hierarchies.

Revolt is the fourth major theme of *The Soft Machine* and is portrayed both through narrative fantasy and in cutup collage passages. In fantasy, revolt is achieved through time-travel and identity change, which is accomplished by the subversive use of orgasm-death and the drug yage. The individual in fantasy can control sex, drugs, and time in order to be free of his body. He can choose a particular body and identity to inhabit instead of submitting to the manipulation of external forces. This autonomous individual can sabotage the "control machine" from within the power system. But he can only do so with the help of technicians or by learning the techniques of control himself. The "machine" of the narrative fantasy is a word-and-image system: reality is a film, identity a script, and the body is behavioristically programmed through visual and auditory stimuli. Revolt is achieved by turning the machine against itself through newspaper cutups, film cutups, photomontage, and synaesthesia. The writer, then, is the chief technician, often understanding the machine better than the rulers who use it for their personal benefit.

"The Mayan Caper" narrates most clearly the process of time travel, identity change, and sabotage; but revolt is portrayed numerous times in *The Soft Machine* in briefer narrative and cutup passages. Imagery associated with revolt is the same as the imagery of the Nova Police: winds, waves, silver, gray, panpipes, dust, silence, and images of disintegration (melting, fading, falling, explosions). Revolt is also associated with the characters of Nova technicians and agents: the Technical Sergeant, Technical Tillie, Iam, the Subliminal Kid, Agent K9, Lee, Clem Snide. Calls to revolt by "partisans" in the fight against the Mob become repeated motifs and metaphors for freedom: "wise up the marks," "storm the reality studio," "smash the machine," "seize the Board Books," and "Word falling—Photo falling—Breakthrough in the Grey Room."

The Nova mythology is not yet fully developed in *The Soft Machine,* and the theme of revolt is limited by the ambiguity of the novel's narrators and of the apocalyptic passages produced by revolt. The "I" of *The Soft Machine* is constantly changing identity, sometimes playing conman and controller, sometimes playing victim or guerrilla. Only the hustler's voice remains fairly constant, but that is a voice that stands for no stable identity or point of view. The writer-persona does not dominate the narrative, and when he does appear, he is more often a passive observer than a rebel, striking out at the controllers only in "The Mayan Caper." As observer, the writer voyeuristically partakes of the evil he condemns: he is the amoral technician who can serve both rulers and rebels. The collage passages of apocalyptic disintegration produced by the writer-technician are also ambiguous: the random action of cutups destroys the current structures of reality and ends history, but the ensuing chaos seems to be a *Götterdämmerung* that liberates no one. *The Soft Machine* is a first experiment with the cutup as the basis for a novel: the cutup analyzes existing structures and breaks them up but does not produce a new order.

Space Travel in *The Ticket That Exploded*

The Ticket That Exploded continues the basic montage/collage form of *The Soft Machine,* but carries the experiments with cutup and mythology much further. This second novel of the trilogy makes more extensive use of cutups and develops the Nova mythology more explicitly and at greater length, leading to the inclusion of expository passages that were not present in *The Soft Machine.* In *The Ticket That Exploded* Burroughs exhibits a technical control that is not attained in the previous novel. The cutups are often effective and moving prose poems, and the increased prominence of the Nova mythology gives the work a coherence and structure that balances the fragmentation of the cutups. Cutups also become meaningful as narrative elements since they play a part in the plot of the myth.

The Ticket That Exploded evolves from *The Soft Machine* and contains much of the same materials, but creates its own fictional world through different thematic emphasis. Whereas *The Soft Machine* concentrates on an analysis of past control of mankind through sexuality, *The Ticket That Exploded* concentrates on mind control in the present through word and image systems. *The Soft Machine* is dominated by South American imagery and anthropological approaches to myth, while *The Ticket That Exploded* is dominated by Moroccan and outer-space imagery and the creation of new myths in science-fiction forms. In *Ticket* Burroughs makes use of the science-fiction convention of portraying the present in a fiction about the future, a purpose clearly announced in the very first routine: "I am reading a science fiction book called *The Ticket That Exploded*. The story is close enough to what is going on here . . ." (TTE, p. 5).[7]

Mind control through language ("word and image locks") is the dominant theme of *The Ticket That Exploded,* and this theme is associated primarily with imagery of machinery, technology, science, and space travel. A secondary cluster of Moroccan images is also associated with the language theme. Since control by the word and image "machine" and liberation from that control both depend upon "technology" (understanding and manipulating the symbol system) some of the same images represent both control and liberation. Interpretation depends upon the context. For example, a "camera gun" may be used by either "force."

The most prominent technological and scientific images are the following: space travel, encounters with fantastic new beings and environments on other planets, the film and its script, the tape recorder and its tape, the camera, the radio and radio static, the electronic switchboard, electrical charges, the pinball machine, the typewriter (which types or punches the script-ticket), laboratory experiments and operations on human subjects, viruses and immunization, addiction and apomorphine. Character-images associated with the language control machine are the Nova Mob characters, Bradly and Lykin—the twin astronauts, a film producer and his sycophant, and the old doctor. The Nova police are associated with dismantling the machine; and aggressive partisans, patrols, and combat troops are added to the more passive agents, inspectors, supervisors, and technicians. Moroccan characters—Hassan i Sabbah and Arab street boys—are associated with liberation from word and image control and are linked to space travel fantasies of fish boys and frog boys. Imagery of the

Moroccan landscape (panpipes, mountains, blue sky, wind, and mist) is often linked to the liberation imagery of the Nova Police (flutes, tornadoes, blue mist, silence, disintegration) and sometimes to the power imagery of Minraud (Minraud is a hot, desert place). For Burroughs, the body is associated with time and the mind with space, so the mind control theme dictates futuristic space travel imagery in *Ticket*, in contrast to the earthbound time travel of *Soft Machine*.

Sexuality remains an important secondary theme in *Ticket*, and the vegetable-Venusian sexual imagery is present. Some of this imagery is used to create outer-space fantasies of the carnival city of sexual victimization, portrayed as the garden of delights (GOD), the exhibition, and the amusement park. Brief narratives portray explorers on earth and in space being taken over by diseases of sexual control: Ward Island disease, the Sex Skin habit, the Happy Cloak, the Other Half. Three extensive cutup collages are devoted to the sexual theme. The outer-space exhibition and amusement park are the basis for extensive collage in the seventh and eighth routines, "writing machine" and "substitute flesh." A collage of lyrics from popular love songs forms the fourth routine, "do you love me?" The latter cutup of love lyrics is a pop-art tour de force using the cutup technique and a form of popular art to criticize the concept of romantic love. The most prominent characters associated with the sexual theme are Bradly as traveler-victim and the predatory seducers, Johnny Yen and the Orchid Girl.

Like *The Soft Machine*, *The Ticket That Exploded* conveys its meaning through a combination of image clusters and narrative episodes. In *Ticket*, one narrative dominates the whole work, appearing in fragments of action and exposition: the Nova mythology. The focus on mind control in this novel and its association with space and technology imagery make possible a further development and use of the Nova narrative. And, through the Nova mythology, Burroughs is able to subordinate the themes of sex, addiction, and power to the theme of language, giving the second novel greater unity. Thus writing and cutups become more important than in *The Soft Machine*, and Lee the agent-writer plays a larger role. Furthermore, as Burroughs develops his theory of the cutup and its role in the Nova myth, cutups point toward something beyond chaotic destruction. The theme of revolt becomes the more positive theme of liberation, and sheer anarchy is replaced by the ideal of autonomy.

The Ticket That Exploded explicitly narrates the plot of the Nova Mob and the Nova Police, with particular emphasis on the Venusian plot called Operation Other Half, in which the Word (language) is used to define and control sexuality (the body). The story is of the invasion of planet earth by the Mobsters and their mechanism of vampirelike possession, transformation, and control. *Ticket,* however, minimizes the gangster and vampire metaphors and develops the virus and film metaphors—which are in keeping with the science and technology theme of the novel. The double metaphor of virus and film provides the controlling imagery for the Nova plot in *Ticket.* Operation Other Half is defined as a double virus invasion: "There were at least two parasites one sexual the other cerebral working together the way parasites will" (TTE, p. 144). The replication of a virus is equated with the linear repetition of the same image. Thus the Other Half is a "disease of the image track" in which human victims are forced to participate in "the reality film," a linear repetition of the same scripts, images, and sounds with no alternative allowed—indeed no alternative is conceivable. The Word virus controls our concept of reality and imposes a dualism that makes it impossible to change reality. Burroughs attacks all either-or thinking, especially the separation and opposition of mind and body, word and world, birth and death, pleasure and pain, male and female. It is these concepts, according to Burroughs, that trap us into bodies that can be manipulated by power elites. The primary form of control is a sexuality in which the Other Half is a yearning for another body to assuage the feeling of separation caused by dualism:

The human organism is literally consisting of two halves from the beginning word and all human sex is this unsanitary arrangement whereby two entities attempt to occupy the same three-dimensional coordinate points giving rise to the sordid latrine brawls which have characterized a planet based on 'the Word,' that is, on separate flesh engaged in endless sexual conflict—The Venusian Boy-Girls under Johnny Yen took over the Other Half, imposing a sexual blockade on the planet— (It will be readily understandable that a program of systematic frustration was necessary in order to sell this crock of sewage as Immortality, the Garden of Delights, and *love*— (TTE, p. 52)

To Burroughs, the Other Half we yearn for—whether seen as the physical pleasure of orgasm, the sentimental feeling of love, the opposite sex, or another body—is an illusion, an image created by Word that is part of a repetitious reality film controlled by external forces. Thus, says Burroughs, Word is the Other Half.

Dualistic thinking sets up a desire for unity that can never be fulfilled because opposites can never become one; at the same time, it creates and aggravates conficts through polarization. The only unity possible in such a mental universe is the victory of one "half" over another, but this is death or Nova. A universe of irreconcilable opposites in conflict is the Nova plot:

> The basic nova technique is very simple: Always create as many insoluble conflicts as possible and always aggravate existing conflicts—This is done by dumping on the same planet life forms with incompatible conditions of existence—There is of course nothing "wrong" about any given life form since "wrong" only has reference to conflicts with other life forms—The point is these life forms should not be on the same planet—Their conditions of life are basically incompatible in present time form and it is precisely the work of the nova mob to see that they remain in present time form, to create and aggravate the conflicts that lead to the explosion of a planet, that is to nova— (TTE, pp. 54–55)

The Nova Police combat this plot through a double metaphorical action: exposure, which produces immunization to deception (the virus-apomorphine metaphor), and cutups which produce a wordless silence (the technology metaphor of film and tape). When the Nova plot is seen as a virus, seeing and understanding the evil are sufficient to free oneself from it with the understanding that regulation of a physical need is the goal, not eradication: "*Communication must become total and conscious before we can stop it*" (TTE, p. 51). The Nova Policeman combats the virus as an "agent" who trains himself through exposure, tracks down Nova criminals like a private eye, and "arrests" them by exposing their identity and techniques. The Biologic Courts attempt to control the arrested virus-criminals.

When the Nova plot is seen as a reality film and individuals as controlled by a pre-recorded tape, the Nova Policeman becomes a guerrilla fighter who aggressively destroys control "lines," "locks," "molds," and "habits" through cutups with film, tape, and text. Many do-it-yourself passages in *Ticket* instruct the reader in specific cutup techniques in these three media. (The "invisible generation," a previously published essay, appears at the end of the book as an appendix on technique.[8]) Control by word and image is paradoxically destroyed by new arrangements of word and image, the random method of cutups ensuring freedom from external control.[9] From this revolt comes a vision that goes beyond destruction. A new autonomous consciousness is born from the realization that reality is an illusion created by word and image locks: "What is word?—Maya—Maya—Illusion—Rub out the word and the image track goes with it—" (TTE, p. 145). Knowledge of the illusion and how to break it leds to the creation of new realities in the Rewrite Department: "Alternatively Johnny Yen can be written back to a green fish boy—There are always alternative solutions" (TTE, p. 54). The narrative of the fish boy, in particular, is

Burroughs's metaphor for metamorphosis into a new state of being based on new mental constructs.

But Nova Police do not attempt to set up a new world order based on one truth (one Word); they "do their work and go" (like apomorphine[10]), providing a model of resistance and autonomy for others. They are identified with Hassan i Sabbah, founder of the secret assassin cult of the eleventh century, and with Prospero of Shakespeare's *The Tempest*, a magician who voluntarily gives us his power. They produce a "silence" in which words and images exist in a random field or space, uncontrolled by linear concepts (the sentence, plot, time, cause and effect). In this silence all forms and identities disappear, the Police and the Mob included. Burroughs the author becomes identified with this activity, and the novel is his silent space, its form a metaphor for the alternative consciousness the work itself creates. In the final routine, "silence to say goodbye," the disappearance of forms is illustrated as the Nova characters say goodbye, and the text itself disappears into the calligraphy of Brion Gysin.

The Nova mythology allows a great proliferation of narrative fragments since the myth acts as a master metaphor that includes and interprets all of the narratives as secondary metaphors. Even narrative fragments that do not explicitly refer to the Nova plot can be seen as versions or transformations of the basic conflict. Astronaut narratives featuring Bradly and Lykin signify exploration of the symbolic field of consciousness and the possibilities of enslavement, rebellion, or metamorphosis. Explorers taken over by the Sex Skin, Happy Cloak, Ward Island disease, or the Orchid Girl are versions of the Venusian Operation Other Half. The adventures of Arab street boys lead to apocalypse and rescue through transformation. The autobiographical John and Bill, experimenting with their 1920s crystal radio set, are technicians producing cutups. The Board and their Board Books are a three-dimensional, realistic version of the Nova Mob and the Word virus. There is no end to the possible transformations or elaborations, making the myth an open construct. The novel is thus a form open to endless elaboration: its present text is but an arbitrary fragment that can be altered in subsequent editions.[11]

Cutups also proliferate in *Ticket*, opening up narrative "lines" to new associations and transformations beyond the capacity of improvisational fantasy by one author. Juxtaposition through cutup exposes hidden relationships and creates new ones, increasing the number and speed of transformations. Cutups break down conventional boundaries ("lines"), thus creating the possibility of alternative forms and alternative realities. And cutups represent the alternative of a new consciousness, that of a self-regulating autonomous individual free of external social and psychological controls. In *Ticket* Burroughs incorporates into his theory of cutups some of the vocabulary and techniques of Scientology, which he investigated in the early 1960s in London, contemporaneously with the writing of the trilogy. [12] Thus Scientology is added to Reich's orgone theory as a major metaphor for and analysis of control.

Burroughs's exploration and analysis of mind control in *The Ticket That Exploded* reveals a theory of language that is structuralist in orientation, although his method of analysis is metaphorical rather than theoretical or scientific. Like the structuralists, Burroughs sees language as a synchronic system of relationships that is suprapersonal. The subject is a creation of language rather than vice versa. And, in subordinating all other behavior to language, Burroughs parallels the structuralist idea that all aspects of culture can be identified linguistically as symbol systems having the same structure as language. Like the structuralists, Burroughs attacks conventional bourgeois concepts of the self and society, and the belief that these concepts are natural, self-evident, or real. He shows that they are linguistic-social constructs linked to particular economic and political structures, and that a structuralist analysis can free one from unconscious victimization through total awareness and self-consciousness. [13] Burroughs's literary expression of structuralist theory goes a step further than the critical analyses of Lévi-Strauss or Barthes or their followers. Burroughs, through his art, attempts to act upon the linguistic system and change it, thereby acting upon and changing the reader's consciousness. He acknowledges the paradoxical nature of his task (fighting words with words), but maintains a belief in the possibility of individual autonomy.

Apocalypse Now: *Nova Express*

Nova Express, the last novel in Burroughs's experimental trilogy, presents the Nova mythology in its final, most fully developed and coherent form and also focuses on that mythology more strongly through its simplified and condensed structure. *Nova Express* continues to use the montage/collage structure of *The Soft Machine* and *The Ticket That Exploded,* but reduces the number of routines to eight carefully selected groups of narrative and cutup passages. Much of the material had been previously published, and it is apparent that Burroughs chose some of his most successful fragments. The eight routines are further subdivided by subtitles, which usually distinguish different narrative episodes and which separate narratives from cutups, thus providing the reader with thematic and transitional guidelines not present in the two previous novels.

Fewer routines selected from among Burroughs's best work and more explicit organization within routines make *Nova Express* a more concise and more easily comprehensible work, but Burroughs goes further in clarifying his fiction for the reader. *Nova Express* begins with a long exposition that immediately presents and explains the central myth, orienting the reader at the beginning to basic metaphors and conflicts. Expository passages throughout the text explain the mythology and other esoteric references (apomorphine, Reich's orgone theory, Hubbard's Scientology, Burroughs's theory of junk, sense withdrawal tanks, and so forth). The function of cut-up material from literary sources is also clarified since three major works receive the most emphasis: *The Waste Land, The Trial,* and *The Tempest.* Thus *Nova Express* is more self-explanatory than the previous novels.

Also, for the first time, Burroughs arranges his routines in a linear sequence, following the plot of the Nova conflict. This plot proceeds from "wising up the marks" and attempted escape by Nova criminals, to the intervention of the Nova Police and taking the case to the Biologic Court, to a deadlock between opposing forces and Burroughs's final warning. The routines are also arranged in an order of increasing complexity: the first routine is a direct exposition of thesis and plot while the last contains nine cutups, more than any other in the book. As Eric Mottram has said, "*Nova Express* . . . is openly didactic and takes the form of a series of warning scenes, proceeding from Burroughs' understanding of his earlier work and the misunderstanding and rejection of it at the hands of the public and the critics."[14] Also, as Mottram's statement indicates, Burroughs seems to be clarifying his mythology in his own mind as well as the reader's.

In his final version of the Nova myth, Burroughs focuses on the cosmic conflict between the Mob and the Police as the dominating metaphor, giving the conflict a metaphysical emphasis, as opposed to the social and psychological emphasis of the two preceding novels. He returns to the gangster-vampire imagery, the addiction metaphor, and the carny world of *Naked Lunch* for the dominant motifs of *Nova Express,* subordinating his previous analyses of body and mind control, their pseudosciences drawn from Reich and Hubbard, and their image clusters to his own pseudoscience of addiction and the accompanying junk imagery. All of the characters assume carny-world identities and voices, and all are versions of Burroughs's actual identities, past and present. For example, Uranian Willy (the reformed addict), the Subliminal Kid (the rebel technician of the cutup), Inspector Lee (the observer who exposes the truth), Hassan i Sabbah (the prophet whose vision comes from drug and linguistic experiments), and Mob members (Burroughs as addict-hustler and creator of his own victimization) are all roles that Burroughs has played in real life. Thus *Nova Express* is based on a merger of autobiographical experience and a cosmic mythology created out of cultural materials (both popular and literary) external to the self. The implication is, of course, that the self is the source of all mythologies; that the cosmic is personal, history is fiction, life is art, autobiography is legend. In *Nova Express,* the continuing themes of the trilogy coalesce into their most powerful expression, probably because Burroughs returns to the carny world of *Naked Lunch* for the controlling vision.

This last novel in the trilogy also reveals most clearly a system of values that the metaphors represent. In his mythic conflict between good and evil, Burroughs maps out a system of equations and oppositions. Virus is equated with addiction, and addiction equals word, equals linearity, equals cause-effect, equals control, equals reality/fact, equals time, equals order, equals repetition, equals form, equals boundaries, equals convention. And the following values are equated with each other and opposed to the preceding list: immunization, apomorphine, silence, cutups/juxtaposition/field, randomness/spontaneity, regulation/autonomy/liberation, space, chaos, innovation, disintegration, merger, improvisation. (Additional values can be added to this list; these are some of the major concepts found in Burroughs's fiction.) In this value system, based on similarities and differences, Burroughs again shows the structuralist tendency of this thought. Burroughs's mythmaking is also an analysis of myth as a system of regulations, as a second-order language that communicates values, and as a mediation between irreconcilable opposites. His analysis of myth parallels that of Lévi-Strauss,[15] but Burroughs applies his analysis to contemporary Western culture, whereas Lévi-Strauss confines himself to the myths of American Indian tribes.

Because of its brevity and the linear arrangement of routines, *Nova Express* lends itself to a chapter-by-chapter analysis. The first routine, "Last Words," opens with a statement of the essential conflict. Hassan i Sabbah and Inspector Lee of the Nova Police directly address the reader in prophetic tones. Hassan tells us that we have been conned into ignorance and victimization by language itself: "What scared you all into time? Into body? Into shit? I will tell you: '*the word*'" (NE, p. 12).[16] Inspector Lee explains the strategy of the Nova Mob and the only defense: total resistance with apomorphine and silence. "And what does my program of total austerity and total resistance offer *you?* I offer you nothing. I am not a politician. These are conditions of total emergency. . . . I would like to sound a word of warning—To speak is to lie—To live is to collaborate. . . . It is precisely a question of *regulation* . . ." (NE, pp. 14–15). The routine then switches to a monologue by a member of the Mob who describes Mob activities, the Nova plot as outlined in the Board Books, and the Mob's plan to escape when the earth blows up. In this monologue, the character of the Intolerable Kid, or I&I (Immovable and Irresistible), another version of the dualistic Mr. Bradly Mr. Martin, tries to produce a Nova by aggravating existing conflicts. But the narrator feels the heat closing in and the marks wising up, and soon the entire Mob is confronted with the possibility of arrest through "total exposure" by the Nova Police.

"So Pack Your Ermines," the second routine, describes the "capers" of a number of Nova criminals, usually ending in intersection and arrest. These capers are cutup with time travel based on Burroughs's autobiographical memories of St. Louis, South America, and Morocco. The routine ends with a "breakthrough in the grey room," both forces trying to seize control of the reality film governing the earth. *Nova Express* again uses the repeated refrain "Word falling—Photo falling—Breakthrough in the Grey Room" to signal the disintegration of present reality. The deadlock results in silence: "The silence fell heavy and blue in mountain villages—Pulsing mineral silence as word dust falls from demagnetized patterns" (NE, p. 40). In the milieu of silence, Agent K9 is transported in time to the past—St.Louis and Dr. Benway. Benway is involved in one of his infamous experiments and explains why junk is blue rather than green (metallic rather than vegetable). He is intersected by the Nova Police, a force in the present. In silence, the past, present, and future merge into one moment; and, when the Nova Police arrest Nova criminals of one time, the criminals of all times are affected.

"Chinese Laundry" increases the suspense of the conflict between the deadlocked forces. "Breakthrough in the grey room" means that Nova is imminent; and, in order to prevent it, the police must discover the apomorphine formula, which will "deactivate all verbal units and blanket the earth in silence" (NE, p. 47), thus counteracting the Nova formula. Once verbal units are disintegrated, Nova cannot take place because the structure that produces Nova will no longer exist. Apomorphine is defined as "no word and no image" and "anti-virus." A Nova Policeman and the District Supervisor interrogate a technician who, under the pressure of interrogation, metamorphizes into Dr. Benway, then into a Death Dwarf. These criminals maintain that the police will never get the formula in time, that "the nova formulae cannot be broken, that the process is irreversible once set in motion" (NE, p. 48). But the defection of Uranian Willy tips the scales in favor of the police. The routine ends with a pitched battle ("Towers, open fire") between Nova Police, aided by partisans, and the Nova Mob. The section in this routine called "Coordinate Points" explains mechanisms and techniques of Nova, the function of the Nova Police, and their techniques.

The fourth routine, "Crab Nebula," describes continuing combat on many fronts, again ending without victory for either side. This routine concentrates on analyzing the virus powers and their source, the Crab Nebula. Agent K9 visits the Insect People of Minraud, whose planet is a totalitarian society controlled by pain and fear. Everything is controlled by the Elders, described as bodiless brains: an intricate bureaucracy wired to the control brains direct all movement like a living computer. Great ovens standing at the center of the cities dispose of offenders. Associated with Burroughs's power imagery, the Insect people are the forces responsible for Hiroshima and Nagasaki, the Nazi concentration camps, and the Stalinist purges. They have occupied earth by forming an alliance with the Virus Power of the Vegetable People (i.e., the sexual control of the Venusians). K9 explains the double virus infecting the soft machine (the body) and the dualistic universe of the Word. He shows how to fight the virus or redirect the machine with various kinds of cutups (called "juxtaposition formulae").

In the fifth routine, "From a Land of Grass without Mirrors," the combat continues, and the human body's weakness for addiction is presented as the corollary of the virus powers' invasion of earth. Several narrative fantasies explore the theme of sexual control throughout history, and the counteraction of Nova agents through identity change. The routine ends with a collage passage, "Remember I Was Carbon Dioxide," on the theme of disappearing identity, which is dominated by cutup material from *The Waste Land*.[17] Whereas Eliot's poem laments the loss of myth, Burroughs's cutup celebrates freedom from illusion while acknowledging the pathos of memories of past attachments. In the section called "A Distant Thank You," Burroughs introduces a new metaphor for a new consciousness that would produce a different human nature: the Lemur People. One of man's evolutionary ancestors, the Lemur People are "all affect" and without aggressive instincts. They are what man has rejected in himself in the course of evolution and civilization: "They are of such a delicacy you understand the least attempt-thought of holding or possessing and they are back in the branches where they wait the master who knew not hold and possess— They have waited a long time—Five hundred thousand years more or less I think" (NE, p. 121).

"Gave Proof through the Night" takes the conflict off the battlefield— earth—and into the Biologic Courts for mediation. All of the virus powers are called before a judge who cancels their permits. The decision is appealed to a higher court, but the superior judge is "The Man at the Typewriter" (Burroughs as writer), who refuses to alter the cancellations, and the virus forces disintegrate. Each section of this routine is built around the theme of disintegration, beginning with the sinking of SS *America*[18] and ending with the death of the gods of time-money-junk. Cutups destroy control and create a timeless, bodiless realm. The final sentence indicates that man has himself created the virus power of his addiction: "Mr. Bradly Mr. Martin, disaster to my blood whom I created" (NE, p. 140).

"This Horrible Case" describes the legal conflict in terms of two incompatible life forms, A and B, and the procedure of the Biologic Courts. Each side has a Biologic Counselor, a writer who prepares briefs by creating facts. Two cutups of *The Trial* and the case of life form A are presented as examples of how a brief is written. The cutups emphasize the theme of the biological trap, an unsolvable dilemma. Within the context of *Nova Express, The Trial* is a parallel example of man's victimization by forces beyond his control or understanding. Burroughs's homage to Kafka also emphasizes the increased importance of the writer in this final version of the Nova myth.

The final routine, "Pay Color," begins with the Subliminal Kid, the rebel technician, destroying current reality through exposing the world's population to film and tape cutups of all past and present cultures. The City, a composite of all human civilizations, dissolves, as do human bodies when reality is perceived as an illusion that is one of many ways of organizing experience, but not a privileged one. All that remains is a "silent" world of sensory perception. The transformation to a timeless, bodiless state illustrates the "last words" of Hassan I Sabbah: "Nothing is true. Everything is permitted." (These are his last words because, once they are truly understood, no further words are possible.) The prophet who had exposed evil at the opening of the book announces his cure at the end: freedom through awareness and alteration of consciousness. Subsequent sections portray disintegration and mental freedom over and over through various narrative episodes and image clusters based on liberation motifs. The most prominent allusions to earlier writings are to Eliot's *The Waste Land, The Tempest,* Reich's orgone theory, and Hubbard's Scientology.

Shakespeare's play, especially, establishes a poignant tone for the novel's conclusion with Burrough's use of repeated fragments of the following lines:

> Our revels now are ended. These our actors,
> As I foretold you, were all spirits, and
> Are melted into air, into thin air;
> And, like the baseless fabric of this vision,
> The cloud-capp'd towers, the gorgeous palaces,
> The solemn temples, the great globe itself,
> Yea, all which it inherit, shall dissolve
> And, like this insubstantial pageant faded,
> Leave not a rack behind. We are such stuff
> As dreams are made on, and our little life
> Is rounded with a sleep. . . .
>
> (4.1, 148–58)

Burroughs identifies the Nova police and himself as writer with Prospero, a godlike artist who uses his magical powers to destroy evil but then gives up the power to control others. Prospero's words also reinforce Burroughs's theme of reality as an illusion. The merger of Prospero's farewell and Burroughs's farewell at the end of the novel is an example of Burroughs's poetic power with cutups:

Nothing here now but the recordings may not refuse vision in setting forth—*Silence*—Don't answer—That hospital melted into air—The great wind revolving turrets towers palaces—Insubstantial sound and image flakes fall—Through all the streets time for him to forbear—Blest be he on walls and windows people and sky—On every part of your dust falling softly—falling in the dark mutinous "No more"—My writing arm is paralyzed on this green land—Dead Hand, no more flesh scripts—Last door—Shut off Mr. Bradly Mr.—He heard your summons—Melted into air—You are yourself "Mr. Bradly Mr. Martin—"all the living and the dead—You are yourself—There be—

Well that's about the closest way I know to tell you and papers rustling across city desks . . . fresh southerly winds a long time ago. (NE, pp. 186–87)

It is obvious by the end of the novel that the order of the routines is illusory since the plot does not progress. Linear sequence implied by the existence of a unified plot is undercut by the fact that the conflict between Nova Mob and Nova Police is escalated to higher and higher levels but never really concluded. Upon examination, it becomes clear that *Nova Express* describes a situation, not an action: the criminal conspiracy is but a metaphor for the human condition. *Nova Express* is a prophecy presenting intense visions of what is, not predictions of what will be. Although the warning about an inevitable world holocaust and social collapse is real enough, [19] the novel's apocalyptic tone does not stem from Burroughs's social criticism, but from a spiritual message. The world of conflict and suffering that is our present reality is a fallen world that can be redeemed and transformed by truth, i.e., a correct vision of things as they are.

Burroughs is a radical thinker who challenges the basic concepts upon which Western civilization is built, but he is not a political thinker with a practical program. Therefore, it is not accurate to interpret Burroughs in solely political or social terms and thus to criticize him for proposing no valid political alternative. [20] On the other hand, part of Burroughs's message is the insistence that political and social changes will not bring greater justice or freedom as long as humanity retains the same conceptual framework. [21]

Cosmonaut of Inner Space

Burroughs's trilogy, taken as one work, is an important contribution to the form and theory of fiction. In the trilogy Burroughs develops the experimental techniques he had first introduced in *Naked Lunch*: juxtaposition, collaboration, and pop mythology. The trilogy experiments with these techniques in more extreme form, leading to a radically new kind of fiction and to a new view of artistic creation.

The juxtaposition technique is used not only between short narratives and between sentences, but within narratives and within sentences. Juxtaposition replaces narrative as the dominant form of the novel, and the cutup becomes an important new form of inspiration along with improvisational fantasy. The exhaustive use of juxtaposition through cutups expands the definition of fiction to include nonnarrative prose fragments and sentence fragments, thus challenging the conventions of the novel and the conventions of the prose text. Like *Naked Lunch,* the trilogy is an antinovel and an antibook even on the level of punctuation, dots and dashes replacing the periods of the sentence. [22] Burroughs has frequently quoted Brion Gysin's statement that "writing is fifty years behind painting," [23] and the trilogy does indeed seem to be an attempt to create the literary equivalent of the painter's collage. It is not possible to do exactly the same thing with words, of course, but Burroughs does succeed in creating new techniques of fiction writing, thus increasing the range and potential of the art, and, in the process, challenging our conventional concepts and forcing a redefinition of the genre.

Increased use of juxtaposition also allows for greater collaboration with other artists, for Burroughs can easily cut up the work of others, both living and dead, into his own texts; and the fragmentary form of his montage/collage novel structure is always open to additional material. Burroughs had remarked upon the organizational and editorial help he received from others in preparing the final text of *Naked Lunch,* but the text itself had been his own composition. In the trilogy, he appropriates the texts of other published writers and actively collaborates with others in creating texts. Collaborations with Michael Portman, Ian Sommerville, Antony Balch, Brion Gysin, and Kells Elvins are duly noted within the novels. Collaboration is another technique that challenges our conventional concepts of the book, the novel, and the literary artist, for we usually regard a novel as the sole product of one shaping and gifted personality.

In the trilogy Burroughs also perfects his use of pop mythology, which becomes not only a form of social criticism but a criticism of the structures of reality (as a form of consciousness that can be altered). Burroughs's mythmaking can be compared to that of many other postromantic artists, but Burroughs's myth is strikingly different from the usual use of a personal mythology to replace outworn traditional beliefs and to give order and informing vision to art. Burroughs's Nova myth is parodic, for, at the same time that it orders experience and creates a world, it satirizes those very functions and negates itself in the very process of creation. Burroughs's myth is not invested with belief; it is not a symbol of transcendent reality. Rather, it is an analysis and criticism of myth whose aim is to destroy the power of myth, leaving the reader free of its linguistic control. Burroughs's desire to destroy myth is the reason his Nova mythology is never really completed or "filled in" with inner detail and final boundaries. It is a fragment that shows how myth is created and how it works without the desire to impose its system upon the reader.

The informing vision of the trilogy is the same hipster mentality that gave *Naked Lunch* its iconoclastic power. The difference is that art (especially the artistic technique of juxtaposition) replaces drugs as the source of vision, and Burroughs becomes more explicit about the fact that he is writing about forms of consciousness rather than the adventures of a particular personality. A theory of consciousness that was implicit in *Naked Lunch* is explicit in the trilogy. For Burroughs, consciousness constructs reality, and no particular system of ordering and comprehending experience is more valid than any other. Every system of thought is a metaphor or myth based on man's linguistic capacity, and every myth is an ephemeral attempt to give form to the formless field of phenomena. Burroughs's novels both illustrate and analyze this human process of structuring and myth-making.

He attacks those who claim a special authority for one vision of reality and celebrates the ability of every person to create his own world. Whereas Hassan i Sabbah's maxim, "Nothing is real: everything is permitted," may strike terror in those who fear the chaos it implies, Burroughs delights in the freedom it gives to play with forms and to create alternative realities.

Burroughs's theory of consciousness is not solipsistic because he acknowledges the prior existence of language and the body and the fact that they shape consciousness rather than vice versa. They are also the means of social interaction and thus the opportunity for evil in Burroughs's world. Linguistic structures and bodily needs can be used to control the consciousness of others. Although Burroughs often expresses in fantasy the desire to be free of both language and the body, his actual position is that mental and physical structures cannot be eliminated but can be beneficially regulated by a consciousness free of external controls.

Burroughs's theory of consciousness and his radical experimentation with form in the trilogy led him to develop his own theory of art as the process of consciousness, and the articulation of this theory in and through the trilogy is probably that work's most significant achievement—both for Burroughs's continuing artistic career and for the history of the avant-garde. The trilogy proposes and illustrates a concept of the artwork[24] as a process and asserts that the goal of art is action rather than contemplation. The art-process, as defined by Burroughs's fiction, begins with the direct apprehension of reality, defined as a conscious mental state. Thus the first task of the artist is to explore psychic territory, a quest undertaken by Burroughs first through drugs, then through note-taking; and, throughout his career, Burroughs has compiled notes on dreams, fantasies, drug-travel-sex experiences, and various social milieus, as well as on his literary experiments. Burroughs himself has defined his purpose as psychic exploration, dubbing himself "cosmonaut of inner space."[25] An individual work is created by selecting, organizing, and editing the notes, which consist not only of current writings by Burroughs but also his past work and that of other artists as well. Using the texts of others and collaborating with contemporaries are part of the process because Burroughs does not see the creating consciousness as separate from other consciousnesses: all art is collaboration.

Publication does not produce the fixed and final form of a particular piece, but a fragment of the continually open and ongoing process of Burroughs's artwork. The process is not complete with publication, and Burroughs's theory does not focus on the art-object as its end. Rather, the goal is the creation of an experience in the reader. Burroughs explicitly states in the trilogy that he wishes to re-create in the reader's mind the experience that his fictions record and embody. The artwork, then, for Burroughs is the lifelong process of consciousness, and individual publications are but fragments of one continuous work. As Burroughs remarked in an interview with Gerard Malanga, "all my books are one book, it's just a continual book."[26] Within this context, Burroughs can and does reuse and revise previously published pieces. Since each work is a fragment of the total artistic process, no work is ever a finished masterpiece immune to change. A publication is an index to the artist's consciousness at that time, but the same work can be revised and placed in a new context later on.

The actual Burroughs artwork is generated by the reader's interaction with the text. A work by Burroughs demands the reader's active participation in the creative process by interpreting a fragmentary text that requires a new way of reading not only the text, but our world. Then the reader becomes one of Burroughs's collaborators in the creation of the artwork, just as we are all collaborators in the creation of reality. Thus Burroughs's insistence that everyone is an artist and that techniques like the cutup can make everyone a poet. Consciousness makes us all creators: Burroughs's artwork is an attempt to reveal this truth.

Burroughs's radical experimentation in the trilogy confirmed his reputation as an important avant-garde artist, and many academic critics of contemporary fiction began to acknowledge his significance in the latter part of the 1960s and in the 1970s. Burroughs was often placed in a 1960s context of existentialism, absurdism, black humor, the antinovel, and radical social protest. Nevertheless, in spite of attempts to see Burroughs as part of contemporary intellectual currents and thus as a serious artist in the modern tradition, his work remained highly controversial. The critical controversy focused on Burroughs's central innovations as a prose writer: the images of sex and violence (what is narrrated), the use of random structures and repetition (how it is narrated), and the ambivalent or contradictory tone (stance of the narrator). Adherents to traditional critical principles tended to reject Burroughs's innovations as morally or artistically reprehensible, whereas critics who were themselves committed to avant-garde art tended to see these very same elements in Burroughs's fiction as the source of his strength and importance as an artist. This clear-cut division of critical response makes Burroughs's work almost a litmus test of a critic's attitude toward the avant-garde.

Reviews of the trilogy were also mixed and often as extreme as those for *Naked Lunch*. Reviewers such as Joan Didion, Theodore Solotaroff, and Terry Southern praised the novels for their insight and technique,[27] while many other reviewers were repelled by the cutup method and by the obscene images that convey Burroughs's analysis of control systems. It is probably true that the average reader has difficulty with the experimentalism of the novels, confining their readership to a special group of admirers (academics, other writers and artists, Burroughs fans). Posterity will decide whether Burroughs's trilogy will be more accessible to future readers, who may find that what was once difficult or eccentric has become yet another familiar convention.

Chapter Four
Utopian Dreams

With the completion of *Nova Express,* Burroughs had exhausted the material from his period of addiction and the textual experiments with cutups. From 1964 to 1971 Burroughs published no new, novel-length books. He was not unproductive, however. He continued to experiment with nonliterary media, to collaborate with other artists, to explore different parts of his own past and present consciousness, and to create imaginary worlds. He published numerous short pieces in a variety of periodicals, many of them in England, where he lived in the late 1960s and early 1970s. Then, in 1971, with the publication of *The Wild Boys,* Burroughs launched a second metaphorical world, which dominates his fiction from 1971 to 1981 and provides the inspiration for the four major works he published during this period: *The Wild Boys, Exterminator!, Port of Saints,* and *Cities of the Red Night.* Two important interviews shed light on Burroughs's second series of fictions.

First published in Paris in 1969, *The Job,* a collection of interviews with Daniel Odier, sums up Burroughs's literary and nonliterary explorations in the 1960s and also points toward the works of the 1970s and 1980s.[1] *The Job* shows Burroughs's continued interest in cutup experiments, nonverbal thinking, hieroglyphics, and current scientific or pseudoscientific research. In his conversations with Odier, Burroughs applauds the youth rebellion of the 1960s, although he remains apolitical, advocating a radical rebellion against basic social structures, such as the nation, the family, and conventional sex roles. He also describes his utopian ideal of an academy to train young people to attain total self-control of mind and body and freedom from external controls. This academy, a "retroactive utopia" set in 1899, is an important motif in Burroughs's subsequent fiction.

The Job includes many short fictions and essays, added after the interviews were completed, so that the final version of the book is just as much a work by Burroughs as it is an interview conducted by Odier. (Burroughs added more new material in the two subsequent editions published in English.) In many ways, *The Job* could be called the quintessential Burroughs book: it is fragmentary; both fact and fiction; a collaborative effort; a combination of old and new, previously published and unpublished material; both improvisational and edited. *The Job* shows Burroughs's artistic process and his definition of art *as* process more clearly than any other work.

The interview with Robert Palmer in *Rolling Stone* in 1972 is also important because here Burroughs announces that his new novel, *The Wild Boys*, represents a significant departure from *Naked Lunch* and the trilogy. He points out that, whereas the earlier novels came from the same body of notes, *The Wild Boys* is based on new material. He also says that all of his current work is related to *The Wild Boys*, suggesting a new series of fictions in the making. Furthermore, he states that he chose to use fewer cutups in the later work, returning to more conventional narrative prose: "I feel that in all those books [the trilogy] there was too much undifferentiated cut-up material, which I eliminated in *The Wild Boys*. The cut-up technique has very specific uses. . . . In *The Wild Boys* I was really quite deliberately returning to older styles of writing. Quite a bit of it is really 19th century. It's a different style of writing."[2]

In the Palmer interview, Burroughs introduces a new element in his evolving theory of the artwork. He puts forth a more aggressive theory of the writer's role as the creator of mental experiences in the reader: "If I really knew how to write, I could write something that someone would read and it would kill them" (RP, p. 49). A theory of art as action dominates the interview: "The future of writing is to see how close you can come to making it happen" (RP, p. 53). This image of the aggressive writer is accompanied by a belief in writing as a necessary medium of communication (and art) that cannot be replaced by other media or symbol systems. When asked if print is on the way out as McLuhan has proclaimed, Burroughs replied, "What does he think is going to take its place? . . . Text is still really essential" (RP, p. 50).

Freedom through Fantasy: A Second Mythology

The publication of *The Wild Boys* in 1971 marked a new direction in Burroughs's writing, characterized by new thematic emphases, new imagery, and a new narrative style. *The Wild Boys* introduces a second metaphorical world, which replaces the Nova mythology of Burroughs's earlier work and which he continues to develop in the following works. The second mythology repeats Burroughs's three major themes—social criticism, the biological trap of sex and death, and the quest of the writer to free himself and his readers from bondage; but the emphasis on politics, on sexual fantasy, and the writer's power is new, as is the attention given to man's positive potential for autonomy, regeneration, and creation.

Burroughs's second mythology, like the Nova myth, is constructed from autobiographical experience and popular culture, but he makes use of new materials from both sources. The most significant biographical material in the later works is childhood memories, and, in particular, the sexual fantasies of adolescence. Thus sexuality becomes the central metaphor of the later works, replacing the earlier addiction metaphor. In the recent fiction, pleasure and freedom through fantasy balance the experience of repression, bondage, and death. Sexual fantasy is linked to artistic creation as a source of and model for fiction—a different but powerful formulation of Burroughs's recurrent thesis that art can be made by everyone and that everyone is an artist. At the same time, Burroughs attaches greater importance to the ability of the *writer,* more than any other artist, to create new worlds and to writing as an art form that cannot be replaced by other media.

Burroughs's most significant use of popular culture in the later works is his imitation of the simple narrative style of popular fiction, especially the pulp fiction he read in his youth. By using the narrative style as well as the characters, images, and actions of the pulps, Burroughs is able to merge his personal fantasies with mass-media fantasies that reach a large public. Thus he appropriates the fantasies of freedom and escape found in the pulps for his own personal and subversive purpose. For no matter how commercialized these fantasies become in the mass media they do express basic human desires for individual autonomy, freedom, and rebirth.

Of course, Burroughs also continues to incorporate new materials from popular culture. The most important new additions are allusions to popular political movements, especially extremes of right and left; youth movements; utopian science-fiction fantasies; and fascination with the occult. Burroughs has read much of the popular occult literature of recent years; and in his fiction he refers to *The Egyptian Book of the Dead, The Tibetan Book of the Dead,* Carlos Castaneda's *Tales of Power,* John Fowles's *The Magus,* and doctrines of witchcraft. This interest in the occult may seem surprising until one realizes that, for Burroughs, the occult is another pseudoscience—like Scientology—that provides alternative realities and good "copy." In his introductory essay to *The Retreat Diaries* Burroughs says,

. . . I am more concerned with writing than I am with any sort of enlightenment, which is often an ever-retreating mirage like the fully analyzed or fully liberated person. I use meditation to get material for writing. I am not concerned with some abstract nirvana. It is exactly the visions and fireworks that are useful for me, exactly what all the masters tell us we should pay as little attention to as possible. Telepathy, journeys out of the body—these manifestations, according to Trungpa, are mere distractions. Exactly. Distraction: fun, like hang-gliding or surfboarding or skin diving. So why not have fun? I sense an underlying dogma here to which I am not willing to submit. The purposes of a Boddhisattva and an artist are different and perhaps not reconcilable. *Show me a good Buddhist novelist.*[3]

The novels themselves reveal that Burroughs's interest in the occult is also related to his belief that the artist is allied with demonic forces within the psyche. *Cities of the Red Night,* for example, is dedicated to all the evil spirits of all the world's mythologies, ending with "To all the scribes and artists and practitioners of magic through whom these spirits have been manifested. /. . . NOTHING IS TRUE. EVERYTHING IS PERMITTED."[4]

Just as in his earlier works, Burroughs combines autobiographical and popular material to create a mythological world that informs all of his fiction from 1971 to 1981. In this second metaphorical world, however, the myth is developed through narrative rather than through cutups. For each of his three major themes—social criticism, the biological trap, and the writer's quest, Burroughs creates a fantasy that becomes one of the major narrative lines in the recent fiction and a metaphor in the myth.

An innovation in Burroughs's treatment of social criticism in the works since 1971 is the creation of utopian alternatives to the present social order so that his satirical fantasies now present both utopias and dystopias in conflict with each other, whereas his earlier fiction had contained extensive portrayals only of dystopias. Burroughs's utopian vision begins in *The Wild Boys* with the futuristic fantasy of "the wild boys"—an adolescent all-male hunting society. This creation evolves throughout the fiction of the next decade, as Burroughs incorporates the wild boys into various utopian and dystopian fantasies.

The wild boys are a metaphorical construct made up of private and public fantasies. The idiosyncratic Burroughs elements are the fantasies of uninhibited adolescent sexuality, the idea of an "academy" for adolescents that teaches individual autonomy and prepares its graduates for guerrilla warfare against the established social order, and an anthropological fantasy on the nature of preagricultural hunting societies. The latter idea was announced in the Palmer interview:

The control machine is simply the machinery—police, education, etc.—used by a group in power to keep itself in power and extend its power. For example: in a hunting society, which can only number about 30, there's nothing that could be called a control machine in operation. They must function effectively as a hunting party in order to survive, so leadership is casual and you have no control machine. Now as soon as you get agricultural society, particularly in rich land, you will tend to get inequality. That is, the advantage of slave labor then becomes apparent and you may have, as with the Mayans and Egyptians, workers and priests—in other words, stratification, repression, and you have a control machine (RP, p. 53)

But the wild-boys fantasy also incorporates the public fantasies of extremist political groups, of the youth revolt, and of the teenage subculture in general. And Burroughs draws upon utopian elements in popular literature, especially science fiction, the occult, self-improvement books, and pornography. The utopian element in the later mythology provides an important contrast to the Nova myth. The Nova myth is primarily pessimistic and stresses the paranoia of much popular thought, whereas the second myth is more optimistic and draws upon the utopian elements in popular political movements.

In his recent work, Burroughs again takes up the theme of the biological trap that makes man susceptible to manipulation by power structures and incapable of transcending the concepts of reality that reinforce social power relationships. He again equates death with sexuality, but the dream erection[5] and orgasm replaces the orgasm-death of the hanged man as the central image and thus gives the basis for visions of transcendence as well as bondage. Burroughs proposes an occult fantasy in which, through conscious control of sex and death, an individual can enter a dream-state of immortality. He can free himself of time, the body and the individual ego. Within this fantasy, orgasm produces transformations in identity which can be controlled by adepts. Metamorphosis thus can be positive or neutral in contrast to the predominantly negative metamorphoses of earlier works. In this new fiction Burroughs seeks to merge the conscious (fantasy) and the unconscious (dream) in an attempt to free, understand, and regulate man's irrational desires. Narcissistic sexual fantasy, popular interest in the occult (and cults), and scientific and pseudoscientific analysis of dreams combine to create a metaphor for immortality. Again, Burroughs uses popular materials to create a utopian ideal.

The theme of the writer's quest in these later works is conveyed by autobiographical images of Burroughs himself as a writer from childhood to the present. Burroughs draws from early parts of his biography and creates an important new character—Audrey Carsons—a version of himself as a child. As this fiction about the writer evolves from *The Wild Boys* to *Cities of the Red Night,* Burroughs gradually incorporates characters from the earlier fiction into the later works and identifies these creations as transformations of the writer who has no one permanent identity. The Lee persona disappears, and the writer persona is less differentiated from other characters. The writer in the new myth has more importance *as* a writer because only writers create stories, that is, narrative, and all fantasy is story; yet he is most aware of the limitations of fantasy. His power to create "reality" is total for his characters, is a powerful model to his readers, but is an endless cycle of bondage to himself—a bondage ending only in death. For the writer of the later works is unable to free himself from his personal and cultural past; nor can he escape the very mental constructs of fiction and reality that allow him to create. He can only show the way for others.

The plot of the myth is again an eternal battle between good and evil, but the opposing forces are now more clearly separated and polarized, leading to simpler images and action as well as to more violence as mutually exclusive realities attempt to destroy each other. More weight is given to the power of utopian fantasy to conquer dystopian reality. The wild boys can finally destroy a repressive civilization simply by ignoring or forgetting it. The individual can enter and control his dreams and thus free himself from his past, his own socially controlled ego, and the bondage of physical existence. Art can produce individual and social freedom, and everyone is an artist in that everyone can create alternative realities and control his own fantasies. The persona of the writer, however, has a limited power that qualifies the myth's simplicity. He is the ego that must remain—no matter how diminished—in order to have consciously controlled fantasy, that is, art; and as long as some ego remains, the reality principle must limit the pleasure principle. Burroughs's utopian fantasies exist in the past or in the future as alternative realities, but never succeed in conquering present reality.

In the works from 1971 to 1981 Burroughs adopts a simplified style based on more straight narrative and fewer and fewer cutups. Plot, characterization, action, and language imitate the narrative style of popular genre fiction, the pulps, and comic books. Many shorter works from this period, such as *The Last Words of Dutch Schultz* (published in London in 1970 but not in the United States until 1975) and *The Book of Breeething* (1975) contain photos and illustrations integral to the text, as if to emphasize the popular parallels. Narrative is also simplified by use of cinematic narrative forms, such as the script and the scenario. Burroughs's new narrative style, however, must be seen within the context of his artistic purpose, just as a Roy Lichtenstein painting must be seen as something more than just a copy of a comic strip. Burroughs's use of simple art forms is part of a sophisticated theory of fantasy and part of a lifelong use of popular forms within an avant-garde context. The simplified narratives exist within in a gradually evolving mythology that is experimental in its "open" construction. Burroughs's myth is never fully organized, coherent, or formally perfect in any way. The stories that make up the myth never wholly fit together. Burroughs's mythology, as always, is a fragmentary process that makes use of the finished products of popular culture to break up the boundaries between reality and fantasy.

The Wild Boys: A Utopian Force

The Wild Boys consists of eighteen relatively brief routines. (All are under twenty pages in length; half are under ten pages.) These routines consist largely of narrative sequences with fewer cutup passages than the trilogy. *The Wild Boys* explicitly tells the reader that the book is a film montage in style and structure, thus clarifying and simplifying Burroughs's film metaphor. Every scene is defined as an ephemeral "set"; every narrative is a "script"; every point of view is a "camera angle"; and every character is an "actor" who frequently changes identities from one narrative sequence to another (as if one film were spliced into another). Cutups are also explicitly presented and framed by the five "penny arcade peep show" segments. And the first "Penny Arcade Peep Show" chapter (WB, pp. 38–49)[6] explains the structure of the book in detail. The novel is like a film theater for an audience of one, showing several narratives simultaneously on several viewing screens surrounding the viewer. At times the viewer observes the narratives (which he can perceive only one at a time); at times he enters one of them as a character (actor). Sometimes he sees the "structuralized peep show" of arbitrarily juxtaposed fragments. Different segments are connected by arbitrary images (a pinwheel, a Christmas-tree ornament, an Easter egg, a copper coil), by punctuation symbols, by captions and images from an old book, or by titles.

The settings, characters, and images in *The Wild Boys* are a combination of new and old creations. Most of the new material consists of memories of Burroughs's childhood in the St. Louis of the 1920s and the new fantasy about the Moroccan wild boys. Some of the characters from Interzone reappear, along with Mexican and Mayan materials, but the variety and complexity of people and places is far less than in the previous novels. Characters remain flat and interchangeable; and, in particular, the first person is used for several different roles, not just that of agent of resistance. The simplicity of character and image, combined with the explicit film

metaphor, makes *The Wild Boys* a more accessible book than the works in
the trilogy and establishes parallels with popular narratives such as comic
books. But the corresponding demand upon the reader to see every narrative fragment and every personal identity as a transitory artifice or illusion
requires a sophisticated reading of an apparently simple narrative.

The Wild Boys introduces all three major themes of the new mythology:
social control versus revolt, the biological trap versus immortality, the
writer's simultaneous freedom to create (and destroy) and his bondage to
the past. These themes are presented primarily through the stories about
the wild boys and Audrey Carsons. Other characters, both old and new,
serve mainly as vehicles for social satire.

The story of the wild boys is the dominant narrative in the novel (hence
the title), and thus makes revolt the dominant theme. The wild-boys story
is a science-fiction fantasy set in the near future in which Burroughs imagines a breakdown of the current social order. Large portions of the Western
world have reverted to savagery and chaos, and what remains of our civilization exists within walled enclosures where an elite rule through a totalitarian police state. The character of the future dystopia is based on the
middle-class, middle-aged, midwestern America of Burroughs's youth,
represented by the interminable racist bore, Colonel Greenfield. This dystopia is opposed by the wild boys, who are a utopian force: a tribe of youth
without leadership or hierarchy. They are both an escape from a repressive
civilization to a fantasy world of endlessly gratified desire, and a world-
wide guerrilla force that recruits and trains youth to fight the totalitarian
social order. The wild boys represent an intentional psychological and social regression; they evade the social controls that underlie our civilization:
concepts of God, country, family, and sexuality. The wild boys' manifesto
says:

> We intend to march on the police machine everywhere. We intend to destroy the
> police machine and all its records. We intend to destroy all dogmatic verbal sys-
> tems. The family unit and its cancerous expansion into tribes, countries, nations
> we will eradicate at its vegetable roots. We don't want to hear any more family
> talk, mother talk, father talk, cop talk, priest talk, country talk, *or* party talk. To
> put it country simple we have heard enough bullshit. (*WB,* pp. 139–40)

The imagery and actions that describe the wild boys define them as
embodiments of demonic energy. Physically they are young, naked males
continually engaged in sex, violence, *and* practical jokes. Like traditional
devils, they combine depravity and malicious glee. The wild boys are the

demonic evil of repressed desire in our culture. They give free rein to the instinctual drives of *eros* and *thanatos* in forms society calls perverse and criminal, existing either in a chaotic whirlwind of murderous violence and orgiastic lust or else in the sated, drugged languor of fulfilled desire. They are savages in their totemistic organization into hunting packs, in their mutilation of corpses and cannibalism, and in their ritualistic use of drugs and sex to control the forces of life and death. They display the demonic behavior of the tribe living a dream-life beyond good and evil in which the individual has no consciousness that separates him from the group. The wild boys are immortal, for they have found the secret of bringing the dead back to life through orgiastic cult practices; hence they are free of parents, women, birth, and death. They exist in a state of ecstasy, represented by their enigmatic, dreamy smiles when they contemplate their actions, a smile that invites ironic comparison with the smile of Dante's Beatrice and of the Mona Lisa—two hallowed female icons that embody traditional Western values. In Burroughs's futuristic fantasy the image of a smiling boy becomes a popular icon that subverts the social order by recruiting more wild boys. This image of the smiling boy and its effect on others (creating more wild boys) is also a metaphor for Burroughs's own subversive pop-art technique and expresses his belief that art can change consciousness to produce action.

The satanic immortality of the cult, the savagery of the tribe, the perverse gratification of instinctual desire, and the naked male body define the wild boys as embodiments of demonic energy; and it is as energy that they are best understood, not as characters. They are utopian as a *force,* not as literal images of the ideal community. (Within the total fiction of this novel and the works that follow, they are a force that combats totalitarian repression.) The wild boys represent the release of demonic energy in conscious fantasy, which Burroughs believes is a means of human liberation—both personal and social. By bringing the unconscious irrational desires of the individual and the group to consciousness and by playing with these forces in artistic structures, Burroughs seeks to free, understand, and regulate man's irrational desires. From this conscious playing with demonic energy Burroughs believes a new human and a new society can evolve. *The Wild Boys,* however, does not describe this new world: it ends on a note of conflict and disintegration as an unidentified narrator attempts to break conventional time barriers and join the wild boys in the fictional future.

The fantasy of the wild boys, as the dominant narrative in the novel, incorporates the immortality theme and the writing theme. The wild boys achieve eternal life and freedom from sexual control, the family, God, and country through their occult ability to control sex and death. They have learned to retain individual consciousness after death and reincarnate themselves at will. The wild boys are contrasted to characters like the boy in "The Dead Child" chapter who cannot control his afterlife because he is still trapped by the "net" of "dead priests and dead gods," i.e., social systems that prevent individual freedom and control. Thus the barrier between the present and Burroughs's futuristic fantasy is not only the predicted collapse of our civilization but the biological and temporal barrier between life and death.

The novel is subtitled "A Book of the Dead," and all of the characters in the novel are dead. The characters who die and who retain consciousness after death—the wild boys, the dead child, Audrey Carsons, and his friend John Hamlin—are part of the immortality theme. Other characters are "dead" because they have never lived; that is, they are fictions created by Burroughs or others and are part of the writing theme. For example, the Mexican characters in the first chapter are part of "an old folklore set," created by Burroughs from cultural stereotypes. Still others are dead because they exist only in the past and are controlled by the writer's consciousness, and one of these dead characters is Burroughs's past self in the character of Audrey. Thus the autobiographical character of Audrey links the writer's quest and the wild-boy fantasy. By fictionalizing his past self and merging that self with another fiction (itself a fantasy arising from Burroughs's consciousness), Burroughs the writer attempts to escape from the bondage of time, the body, and social conditioning. Again, this escape is only suggested at the end of the book, not achieved.

Exterminator!: Writing Death

Burroughs's next major work, *Exterminator!*, continues in the style of *The Wild Boys*: more narrative, fewer cutups, explicit use of the film metaphor, greater simplicity of action and characterization. *Exterminator!* differs from *The Wild Boys* in that the narrative passages and cutups are shorter (most are a few pages), while characters, places, and themes are more numerous, ranging over the whole body of Burroughs's work and giving the book a kaleidoscopic quality. Many of the chapters in *Exterminator!* are previously published pieces that can stand alone as short stories or cutup poems. In fact, although the publisher chose to label *Exterminator!* a novel, Burroughs himself prefers to consider the book a collection of short pieces.[7] But thematic unity allows interpretation of the work as a whole. The major theme throughout is the writer's quest for freedom, and *Exterminator!* is largely devoted to developing this storyline within the second mythology.

In *Exterminator!* Burroughs seems to illustrate in fiction his definition of art as aggressive action: "If I really knew how to write, I could write something that someone would read and it would kill them" (RP, p. 49). The writer in *Exterminator!* is equated with a (vermin) exterminator, a job that Burroughs once held. The exterminating writer kills off all of his characters and destroys their worlds. This "extermination" is singularly mild in its impact upon the reader because the explicit film metaphor and the cartoon level of characterization distance us from the characters and the acts of violence. Each character is an ephemeral image, not a fixed identity, an actor in the film the author has created from his own consciousness and whom he can painlessly destroy.

Furthermore, since all of the characters are presented as versions of Burroughs the writer, Burroughs directs the violence inward, toward himself and his fictions, rather than toward others. The autobiographical Audrey Carsons is described as a child who wants to be a writer and whose first story, "The Autobiography of a Wolf," expresses his fantasies of becoming an outlaw and escaping both social control and human form. Burroughs shows that all of his subsequent characters are transformations of Jerry the wolf, including Audrey himself, who is a later fictional creation. Transformation of characters is accompanied by transformation of stories, as stories within stories are told, ending in death or apocalypse. The ease with which the writer creates, transforms, and destroys his fictions encourages the reader to view "self," "reality," and "time" as equally transitory and illusory fictions, which we have the power to destroy or change. Fictional transformation is equated with immortality.

But the writer cannot finally disappear into his fictions. In the final routine, called "The End," Burroughs portrays a writer whose film is running out but who cannot imagine a life outside the film. Burroughs seems to be acknowledging that, although his art attacks conventional concepts of reality, it is still bound by those conventions. Similarly, Burroughs the man is tied to his temporal, physical existence and cannot be free of his own historical self. *Exterminator!* shows the power of the writer to create and destroy and thus the power of consciousness to play with the structures of reality, but bondage to "present time" remains.

Exterminator! also uses the film metaphor for satirical analysis of social evil. The image of the film running out is used to warn of the imminent collapse of Western civilization, which has been repeating the same script of power and control over the centuries. Both the victims and the controllers have begun to lose faith in the repetitious old film. As Burroughs stated in the chapter entitled "The Coming of the Purple Better One," a routine about the 1968 confrontation between the Chicago police and youthful antiwar demonstrators,

> I have described the Chicago police as left over from 1910 and in a sense this is true. Daley and his nightstick authority date back to turn-of-the-century ward politics. They are anachronisms and they know it. This I think accounts for the shocking ferocity of their behavior. . . . And what is the phantom fuzz screaming from Chicago to Berlin, from Mexico City to Paris? "We are REAL REAL REAL!! REAL as this NIGHTSTICK!" As they feel, in their dim animal way, that reality is slipping away from them. (E, p. 97)[8]

In the final routine, "The End," Burroughs addresses the same stereotyped policemen:

> What kept you doing it Clancy? It was the feeling you were *on set* knowing you had a part in *the film*. . . . And you didn't mind doing these things so long as the film covered you. . . . Well the film isn't there any more Clancy the spring is gone from your sap strength sags from your good right arm cold and wooden your fingers. . . . It was the film held you together, Clancy you *were* the film all the old cop films eating his apple twirling his club. . . . The sky goes out against his back. (E, p. 164)

In this passage, Burroughs not only satirizes a type of controller but also those who become totally identified with their stereotyped social role. When the role they have played becomes outdated, these "actors" feel a loss of identity. In Burroughs's satire a person who has become one with a stereotype may even be in danger of losing his very existence when the stereotype dies.

The style of Burroughs's satire in *Exterminator!* returns to the broad humor and outrageous obscenity of his earliest routines, such as "Twilight's Last Gleaming"[9] and "Roosevelt After Inauguration"; and some of his oldest characters and images reappear—the virus, the baboon, the repressive policemen, the man-become-monster. For example, Burroughs's piece on the 1968 Democratic Convention makes brilliant use of the baboon-character, with which Burroughs had attacked Roosevelt's lust for power, in order to satirize the 1968 election and to link his past and present political satire. (The baboon played an important role in the old Benway routines as well.) This return to an earlier style and imagery reinforces Burroughs's point that the power structure is endlessly repetitious in its methods and its goals. Burroughs's satire can thus only repeat itself, exposing the same lies, attacking the same outrages.

Port of Saints: The Art of Narrative

Port of Saints (1975), the last major work Burroughs completed before his return to the United States, shows him returning to narrative as the basic form of the novel, for *Port of Saints* consists entirely of stories. Although some of the stories are typical Burroughs routines (satirical fantasies), most are nonsatirical narratives set in an imaginary past or future. For the first time Burroughs becomes a storyteller who develops his imaginary world through narrative transformation (that is, storytelling) rather than through juxtaposition (cutups). These stories are not, however, whole narratives. They tend to be episodes that are part of an implied, but not completed, plot. Also, the stories in *Port of Saints* are not narrated in a straightforward, conventional manner. Burroughs has fragmented the stories into very short passages and shuffled them together. Chapters organize groups of fragments under titles derived from popular song lyrics. The organization of the plot fragments is partly chronological, partly thematic, and partly arbitrary. *Port of Saints* is a collage of stories different in concept and structure from the montage of routines and cutups that provided the structure of Burroughs's novels from *Naked Lunch* to *Exterminator!*

In *Port of Saints* Burroughs further develops his second mythology by creating new stories from new and old material and by linking the stories together. He continues to develop themes, images, characters, and plots from *The Wild Boys* and *Exterminator!*, the most important being stories about Audrey Carsons and the wild boys. He resurrects old characters from his earlier fiction, such as Brad, Greg, and A. J., and he creates many new characters who become important in the mythology: the boys in Harbor Beach, Captain Opium Jones and his crew, and Jerry the carnival boy. South America, Morocco, and the Midwest of Burroughs's youth are the primary settings. Stories are linked as characters from one story enter another and as Burroughs gradually suggests that one of the characters, Audrey the child-writer, is the author of all the stories. Audrey is a reader of pulp fiction (*Amazing Stories, Weird Tales, Adventure Stories*) whose stories are personal fantasies of power and escape that imitate his reading. Thus the source of the stories explains their episodic structure and their popular style.

The most important plot development in *Port of Saints* is the merger of the Audrey Carsons and the wild boys stories in a plot to rewrite history.

In *Port of Saints,* Audrey becomes a wild boy and is part of a guerrilla action by the wild boys to "rewrite all the wrongs of history" through time travel, identity change, immunity from the cycle of birth and death, individual control of sex and dreams, and technological creativity. An example of how to rewrite history is given in the second chapter, "Numero Uno." The wild boys travel to a West Indian island in the year 1845 and act as technical advisers to black guerrillas fighting Portuguese and British colonialists. Using raw materials, technology, and knowledge available at the time, the wild boys invent a grenade and a gun that are technologically superior to existing European weapons, enabling the guerrillas to massacre the British troops sent to suppress the rebellion. The secret of their success is not present knowledge transported to the past, but inventive thinking that goes back to the beginning of firearms (the firecracker) and constructs weaponry on entirely different principles from the technology of existing weapons. The wild-boy intervention in the West Indies changes not only political history but technological history: science fiction changes the present by changing the past. This new plot development in *Port of Saints* and the numerous new narrative episodes that appear in this book stress the freedom-through-fantasy theme as both Audrey and the wild boys escape the past (both personal and historical) and the biological trap (the cycle of birth and death).

Cities of the Red Night: Retroactive Utopia

Cities of the Red Night (1981) is a culmination of Burroughs's second mythology of freedom through fantasy. Burroughs attempts in this novel to expand his mythological narratives to include the entire earth, all of its peoples, both sexes, and all of human history. The length and style of *Cities* also imply the intent to portray an all-encompassing mythology. *Cities* is longer than any other Burroughs novel (over 300 pages) and contains more sustained narrative. Furthermore, the book's three interrelated plots thoroughly develop the three major themes of Burroughs's second myth. A retroactive utopia founded by eighteenth-century pirates is the basis for Burroughs's social criticism. A story about the dystopian cities of the red night focuses on the theme of the biological trap. And the writer's quest is conveyed through a contemporary detective story in which a private investigator uncovers the biological trap and finds he must rewrite history to escape it.

In *Cities of the Red Night*, as in *Nova Express*, Burroughs constructs a comprehensive pop mythology that uses popular materials to critique present reality and also to create alternative realities. Each of the three major plots is drawn from an easily recognized popular genre. The pirate's retroactive utopia is based on boys' adventure stories; the prehistoric cities are based on popular science and science fiction; and the contemporary mystery is based on hardboiled detective stories. All three plots also use occult elements drawn from popular literature and beliefs. Divided into three books, with alternating yet interrelated plots of suspense, *Cities* imitates the structure of popular thrillers, such as those written by Frederick Forsyth, a writer Burroughs admires,[10] and also of the popular "triple deckers" of earlier centuries. Burroughs further conforms to popular conventions in his sustained use of the flat narrative style of popular genre fiction. The pirate story is told in diary form and in the pedestrian style of the non-professional writer. The detective story imitates the hardboiled, factual style of the cynical private eye. The cities story alone makes use of Burroughs's characteristic parodic style, but all three stories take popular narratives as their inspiration, with the emphasis on narrative art, or storytelling. Of course, Burroughs's stories are not strictly imitations of popular stories; they all contain typical Burroughs themes and motifs, which transform the popular into the avant-garde.

Cities of the Red Night creates a science-fiction myth that explains all of human history as we know it and an alternative history that shows the power of fantasy. The cities of the title are an imaginary, prehistoric civilization portrayed in a science-fiction mode that satirizes contemporary Western society. The cities are a dystopia set in the past but mirroring the present. These prehistoric cities are also the source of the B-23 virus,[11] a metaphor for the biological trap of sex and death. This virus in present time sets in motion a contemporary detective story that is gradually transformed into the writer's attempt to free mankind from bondage to the past. Burroughs contrasts his dystopian vision of the cities of the red night and their disastrous legacy to the present with a retroactive utopia that universalizes the wild-boy fantasy. He transforms the wild-boy plot to rewrite history into the story of a libertarian pirate society in eighteenth-century South America that overthrows Spanish rule and changes the course of history. The citizens who subscribe to "the Articles" of liberty fight a continual guerrilla war against the nation state and its methods of control. They create a society of small communes, loosely federated to share technology, expertise, and defense. This anarchist utopia is projected into present time, based on its imaginary historical origin. Thus Burroughs's dystopian cities and utopian communes are placed in conflict in the present as metaphors for opposing forces in contemporary society, and the writer-detective must resolve the conflict.

Burroughs is not content with simply telling a story, however. Rather, he wants to show the reader the power of storytelling and, in particular, the power of fantasy in all senses of the word. Although book 1 begins the novel in a relatively conventional manner by introducing the three plot lines and developing each one separately, Burroughs never goes on to complete these stories. In books 2 and 3, plot development becomes episodic, fragmented, and chaotic. The storylines remain open and unfinished with many gaps, part of another fragmentary mythology like the Nova myth of the earlier works. Just as Burroughs's trilogy showed the reader how to destroy old myths with cutups, *Cities of the Red Night* shows the reader how to create alternative realities with material at hand and with the human ability to dream and to tell stories. Burroughs wants to stimulate the reader to create his own stories, not to present him with a finished story for his passive consumption.

Not only does Burroughs refuse to complete his stories in books 2 and 3, he also merges his three narratives in an unconventional manner in order to emphasize their fictionality. Characters, actions, and images from one story appear in another; characters and narrators merge and shift identities as they enter different narratives; time and space merge so that all three stories seem to be taking place in a past that is also the present and the future. Each story becomes reflexive as, in each case, a character within the story is revealed to be the writer of the story, and each writer merges with his own story in a circular pattern. The most important merger is that of the heroes of the three plots, each of whom is a quester for knowledge and a writer. Noah Blake of the retroactive utopia merges with Clem Snide of the detective story, who merges with Audrey—a wild boy in the cities story. In the final chapters, the entire novel is collapsed into the consciousness of the adolescent Audrey, who has either dreamed or written it all. In the penultimate chapter, "We Are Here Because of You," the structure of the novel is compared to a high-school play taking place in "a vast loft-attic-gymnasium-warehouse" containing all possible costumes, props, and sets, and in which many performances are going on "at the same time, in many rooms, on many levels." Fiction and reality thus portrayed is a world of possibility, illustrating again Hassan i Sabbah's maxim, "Nothing is true. Everything is permitted."

But Burroughs does not conclude with this vision of total freedom through fantasy as the artist merges with his fiction. Instead, he concludes with a return to Port Roger, the eighteenth-century pirates' base. An unidentified narrator in the persona of the elegiac writer qualifies the fantasy:

> I have blown a hole in time with a firecracker. Let others step through. Into what bigger and bigger firecrackers? Better weapons lead to better and better weapons, until the earth is a grenade with the fuse burning. . . . A few may get through the gate in time. Like Spain, I am bound to the past.[12]

As in all of Burroughs's major works, the cosmic conflict remains unresolved: the author, the narrators, and the reader are left with the need for eternal vigilance and struggle.

"It Is Necessary to Travel"

In his fiction from *The Wild Boys* to *Cities of the Red Night* Burroughs continues to be an innovator who combines prophetic visions and experimental technique. He creates powerful imaginary worlds that critique present reality and that show the reader how to alter his consciousness and thus his world. He continues to produce fragmentary fictions within the hipster's concept of the artwork, which was elaborated in the trilogy and outlined in chapter 3 of this book. The works from 1971 to 1981 are "all one book," and Burroughs overtly ties the later works to the earlier fiction by incorporating old material into his new creations.

Burroughs's second series of fictions, however, does modify his theory and practice in significant ways. The works imply the following theoretical assumptions. First, Burroughs emphasizes the importance of writing as opposed to other forms of art because only writing can create alternative worlds. The writer's power to *create* experiences for the reader replaces Burroughs's earlier idea that the artist *re*-creates in writing a nonliterary psychic experience. Burroughs now adopts a performative rather than a mimetic theory of art. Psychic exploration occurs within his fictions, not outside them. The goal of producing an experience in the reader, of changing his consciousness, remains the same, but the experience is now created by the text through mental structures that only texts can create, that is, through narrative.

Whereas the trilogy experimented with nonnarrative fiction, the works since 1971 have returned to the origins of fiction: storytelling. Only through narrative does writing differ from other art forms, and only through narrative are alternative worlds created. In *Naked Lunch* drugs were the source of vision; in the trilogy cutups gave insight; in the works after *The Wild Boys* narrative is vision. Thus the sources of art—dream and fantasy—are equated with storytelling, and writing and books become metaphors for the structures of consciousness. In *Cities of the Red Night,* for example, the control machine is a book, and it can be dismantled by rewriting the book; and utopia is attained not by trying to imagine an ideal future but by rewriting history to produce a different present.

Burroughs's use of narrative does not mean a return to conventional forms of fiction, however. His works remain fragmentary in structure because he wishes to explore the power to create stories rather than to tell particular stories. In fact, Burroughs's second mythological world is even more open-ended and heterogeneous than his first. The Nova myth supplied a single metaphor incorporating every image, character, or action that Burroughs chose to include in his text. The myth of freedom through fantasy is a mental construct that produces many metaphors and no one controlling metaphor, for all stories in this myth are of equal importance, and all stories are capable of infinite transformations. Furthermore, Burroughs's storytelling becomes reflexive in his emphasis on the fictionality of his stories and on the writer writing what the reader is reading. The reader is always made aware that Burroughs's stories are fictions, and he is encouraged to "see through" all of the fictions that order experience. Burroughs again demands active participation from the reader in the process of the artwork, and again equates the artwork with consciousness itself. His lifelong exploration of "inner space" remains open-ended: "This is the Space Age. Space is a dangerous unmapped area. It is necessary to travel. It is not necessary to live."[13]

Burroughs has continued to travel as an artist, but few critics have traveled with him. His work since 1971 has received less attention than *Naked Lunch* and the trilogy, and reviewers have been more negative. Of the four works discussed in this chapter, *The Wild Boys* has received the most positive reception. Josephine Hendin and Alfred Kazin praised the novel for its exploration of the psyche and its social criticism.[14] John Tytell called *The Wild Boys* Burroughs's best book since *Naked Lunch* because of its powerful fantasy of revolt.[15] Other reviewers of *The Wild Boys* and the majority of the reviewers of *Exterminator!* and *Cities of the Red Night* professed disgust and boredom with Burroughs's characteristic imagery and fragmentary technique. Thomas M. Disch's tirade on *Cities* is representative:

Forget morality! Forget art! What Mr. Burroughs offered the rubes back in 1959 and what he offers them today, in somewhat wearier condition, is entrance to a sideshow where they can view his curious id capering and making faces and confessing to bizarre inclinations. The backdrops are changed every few minutes by lazy stagehands, but the capering id delivers an identical performance before each one. It's grotesque, it's disgusting, but gosh—it's real! Readers who have never caught Mr. Burroughs's act would do better to read "Naked Lunch" than this rather anemic clone.[16]

Reviewers like Disch echo the early criticism of *Naked Lunch* ("Ugh!") with the additional fillip that they are now bored, rather than shocked, by Burroughs's obsessions. Several reviewers of *Cities* also expressed disappointment because Burroughs began stories but did not complete them.[17] Recent reviewers in general have shown a lack of understanding of Burroughs's purpose and technique. Some expressed their reservations with restraint, acknowledging Burroughs's seriousness as an artist, but no enthusiastic proponents have rated these later works as highly as *Naked Lunch* and the trilogy.

As this chapter has shown, Burroughs's work since 1971 deserves far greater attention and respect than it has heretofore received. These works extend Burroughs's achievement as an innovator, as a creator of powerful visionary fantasies, as a satirist, and as a pop artist. Contrary to the reviewers' complaints about repetition, Burroughs has grown as an artist in this period, exploring new materials and techniques. The recent *Cities of the Red Night,* in particular, represents a new technical departure. Of the four works discussed in this chapter, *The Wild Boys* and *Exterminator!* are solid achievements using Burroughs's montage/collage structure with greater clarity to portray a new mythological fantasy, contemporary political satire, and a writer's meditation on his art. These two works, taken as individual works, are more accessible and emotionally powerful than any single volume in the trilogy, and they almost attain the mastery of *Naked Lunch*. *Port of Saints* and *Cities of the Red Night,* because of their recent publication[18] and their surprising experimentation with narrative, are more difficult to evaluate. Technically they represent a major innovation in Burroughs's artwork and open up many possibiities for the future. The extended use of a simplified narrative style in these works, however, reduces the visionary power of Burroughs's fantasies.

During the decade 1971 to 1981 Burroughs also published many shorter pieces and gave many interviews that are part of the artwork of this period. Since his return to the United States he has published several additional books, some of which were previously published in England and some of which are new creations. *The Third Mind* and the complete *Junky,* mentioned in previous chapters, are important publications of earlier work. (The 1977 Penguin edition of Burroughs's first novel revises the spelling of the title.) New short fiction of importance includes *Cobble Stone Gardens* (1976), a poignant collage about the past dedicated to Burroughs's parents; *Roosevelt After Inauguration* (1979), a collection of brilliant satirical routines on the modern presidency, the antihomosexual crusade, and Christian fundamentalist cults; and *Blade Runner* (1979, no relation to the 1982 science-fiction film based on a Philip Dick story), a short novel that uses a wild-boy hero in a dystopian fantasy about our current crisis in medical care. All three of these works—each entirely different in subject matter and tone—are emotionally and technically successful, showing Burroughs's continued artistic vitality and control. Indeed, the number and variety of Burroughs's publications in the 1970s and early 1980s show that he continues to be productive and innovative. And the Nova Convention, held in Burroughs's honor in New York City in 1978, shows that to some, at least, he is a master.

Chapter Five
Conclusion:
A Mutation in Consciousness

Evaluating the achievement of a living writer is always difficult. In Burroughs's case, contemporary assessment is even more problematic because he is such a constant innovator and because of the critical controversy his work has aroused. Throughout his career Burroughs has always received extreme responses to his work, from "possessed by genius" to "ugh."

Contemporary literary critics, in general, have labeled Burroughs an experimentalist who has introduced new techniques and subject matter into the novel. Although this is no mean achievement, such a view of Burroughs's work severely limits his reputation, giving him the status of a minor novelist outside the main tradition of the genre. Burroughs's importance is thus reduced largely to the impact of one book—*Naked Lunch*, the seminal novel which first presented his major innovations to the public in powerful form. Critics usually see the subsequent novels in the trilogy as lesser works in which Burroughs repeats himself a great deal and in which he turns toward greater obscurity with his cutup technique. They often dismiss the later fiction as even more repetitious and boring. In particular, the reviewers who write for mass-circulation newspapers and magazines have already classified Burroughs as a phenomenon of the past and rarely credit him with any current importance.[1]

This evaluation of Burroughs's achievement is based on an extremely narrow view of his fiction and artistic intentions. As a novelist Burroughs is much more than the author of one important book, and he is the opposite of the type of minor artist who seeks to repeat his achievement in a series of self-imitative works that attempt to recapture his initial success. In fact, Burroughs has continually grown and changed as an artist, producing a number of important novels that revise his central vision and expand his technical repertoire. Furthermore, he has created a new kind of pop-art novel, one that presents a powerful critique of the structures of consciousness and a vision of an alternative reality. In addition, Burroughs must be seen not only as a novelist but as an artist who has created an avant-garde art form that challenges traditional genre distinctions and therefore stan-

95

dards of judgment. An adequate assessment of Burroughs's achievement must be based on an understanding of his "artwork," which redefines the goal and methods of art. In the context of this avant-garde aesthetic, Burroughs's work gives him claim to the status of a modern master.

Burroughs the Novelist

Burroughs's creation of a new novel form—the pop-art novel—is a substantial contribution to the history of the genre, for very few writers have actually created a new literary form. Burroughs's pop-art novels both critique current reality and represent a new form of consciousness in which conventional polarities are seen as part of a field of possibilities. Burroughs creates his vision of a unified culture by including within the literary genre of the novel elements of popular culture that modern urban bourgeois society usually ignores or suppresses: obscene language, description of bodily functions, oral folklore, the manners and mores of "underground" subcultures, and the style of "subliterature."

The "carny world" discussed in chapters 1 and 2 is, of course, the most important subculture included in Burroughs's novels because it provides a worldview: hipsterism. The hip viewpoint of the carny world is a powerful critique of the structures of consciousness in modern bourgeois society. The carny world counters psychological repression with the free expression of sexual and aggressive desires, and counters social conformity and prescribed forms of behavior with spontaneity and improvisation. Morally and aesthetically, the carny world is "the world upside down"[2] because it allows forbidden experiences, parodies established social and artistic forms, and breaks all rules of decorum. The vision of the carny world is also a new reality in which all cultural possibilities exist within one field of consciousness. Psychologically, the repressed coexists with the "permitted" in a merger of Ego and Id. In the carny world "nothing is true and everything is permitted," and consciousness is a process of free play with forms. In this world of total possibility, the individual is an autonomous being who can create a self and a world free of external conditioning.

Burroughs's pop-art vision is the source of his many technical innovations: his use of improvisation and juxtaposition, his destruction of conventional generic categories, his use of collaborative methods and mixed-media techniques, his treatment of character and point of view. These techniques enable Burroughs to ignore the separation between high and low art, literate and oral culture, refined and vulgar manners, and also the conventional barriers between genres, between the media, between individual works of art and individual artists, between artist and audience, and between life and art. Thus Burroughs's various technical experiments in the novel create new forms of authorship, of the text, and of the book, as well as corresponding new concepts of consciousness and reality, self and society. The experimentalism is unified by a vision and a purpose sustained throughout his works.

Seen within the context of the novel genre, Burroughs is a major innovator who carries on the tradition of the modern novel as an avant-garde form. His achievement as an experimental novelist is an important one in that he adds to the genre with originality and power. His pop-art novels are at once a new form, a new vision, and a manifestation of new consciousness. They surpass any comparable work in the literary or visual arts since World War II.

Burroughs the Creator of the Artwork

Burroughs's achievement as a novelist is substantial, but to see Burroughs as a novelist only is to ignore his artistic purpose and much of his work. For Burroughs is the creator of an artwork that ignores genre distinctions. Briefly summarized, Burroughs's artwork defines art as the process of consciousness, which produces a series of fragmentary works whose goal is to change the consciousness of the reader. The artwork demands the active participation of the reader; and, if the reader accedes to this demand, he must, in some sense, alter his consciousness and therefore change his life. The reader then participates in the art process and collaborates with the artist in the creation of the artwork. Such an aesthetic theory can never produce a masterpiece in the conventional sense because it ignores genre and craftsmanship. Thus Burroughs's fiction cannot be judged by the conventional standards applied to masterpieces. Rather, Burroughs's artwork asks to be evaluated according to how well it achieves its own self-defined goal and how well it employs its artistic method.

Burroughs has stated that the goal of his artwork is to change consciousness and thus to change society. A change in consciousness can only occur within the minds of individual readers, and for some readers Burroughs's texts do alter consciousness in the sense defined by the artwork and, therefore, do produce at least moments of psychic alteration. Those moments may or may not trigger a permanent process of change, but Burroughs would surely agree that no artwork can be more than a transitory experience, which may or may not determine subsequent experiences. Burroughs's texts have succeeded with a substantial number of "significant" readers, as shown by the praise of other writers and artists, critics, and Burroughs's appeal to youth. These readers are his target audience, and he has reached them effectively. (His publication in little magazines, underground journals, and in some popular magazines plays a crucial role in reaching his intended audience.) An avant-garde writer such as Burroughs does not aim to reach a mass audience; nor does he try to please conservative literary critics. Furthermore, a writer who tries to change consciousness expects to receive howls of protest from readers who resist change, and the outrage of some readers is itself a sign of effectiveness. Thus the praise of a limited but highly qualified audience is evidence of the success of Burroughs's texts in achieving their psychological goal.

The corresponding change in society, of course, has not been achieved by Burroughs's art in the utopian sense, but he has, as a legendary leader of the Beat movement, had an effect upon contemporary society. The revolt of a few young artists in the 1940s and 1950s became a mass movement in the 1960s and has changed contemporary culture. The hipster mentality has permeated popular culture; and, whether Burroughs is seen as a forerunner or an instigator, his legend has played a role in producing social change. In fact, the legend should be seen as part of the artwork, an aesthetic construct that interacts with the fragmentary texts in a dynamic, evolving process. The legend is Burroughs's art as pure action and, through mass collaboration, merges more thoroughly with popular culture than do his texts alone.

In addition to evaluating Burroughs's artwork according to success in achieving its goal, the artwork can also be judged by its method: the aesthetic criteria created by the work itself. The criteria by which Burroughs's work would judge itself are the following moral values: truthful perception (vision), honesty, courage, persistence, and spontaneity. The works also define these formal or aesthetic values: power (energy), innovation, and humor (laughter, delight). Technically the works require skillful improvisation, collage, and collaboration within expressive forms that are open (free form, fragmentary). It has been the purpose of this book to show that Burroughs's artwork does indeed possess all of these qualities on a consistently high level in not one but many performances. Finally, Burroughs's aesthetic demands that he create an individual style consisting of his own characteristic imagery and forms, for altered consciousness cannot be communicated through existing forms. Furthermore, the style must be not only unique, but one that can sustain continual artistic growth and innovation. Again, Burroughs has succeeded in creating such a style: a fiction by Burroughs is immediately recognizable as his, and he has created his own novel form. Yet he has always kept moving: his most recent novel, *Cities of the Red Night,* is not the same as *Naked Lunch* or even *The Wild Boys* or *Port of Saints.*

Thus Burroughs has achieved notable success in attaining his artistic goal and in meeting the aesthetic criteria created by his own work. And he has maintained a high standard of performance over time. By creating his own art form, which produces its own definition of art, theoretical formulas, and critical criteria, Burroughs allies himself with the international avant-garde that has been an important part of modern art for the past one hundred years.[3] In fact, Burroughs might be called the avant-garde artist *par excellence* for his iconoclasm, originality, and devotion to his ideal.

In a final evaluation of Burroughs's work, then, it should be compared to that of other avant-garde artists. In fact, his artwork is often better understood in the context of painting and poetry rather than of the novel. Pop artist Roy Lichtenstein and action painter Jackson Pollock provide parallels in the visual arts. Burroughs could also be compared to several modern American poets who have written long poems or poem sequences made up of fragments, including T. S. Eliot (who has exerted a profound influence on Burroughs), Ezra Pound, William Carlos Williams, Charles Olsen—and Allen Ginsberg. Burroughs has often said that "writing is fifty years behind painting," and this statement certainly applies to novel criticism versus art and poetry criticism. Pop art in painting has received higher acclaim from critics than have Burroughs's pop-art novels. Similarly, critics have been more ready to accept in poetry the kind of avant-garde techniques found in Burroughs's prose.[4] If indeed *prose* writing and criticism lag behind painting and poetry, perhaps in fifty years William S. Burroughs will be acknowledged as a modern master of the avant-garde.

Notes and References

Chapter One

1. Jack Kerouac, *On the Road* (New York: New American Library, 1957), p. 120. The characters mentioned in the passage are based on members of Burroughs's circle in the 1940s: Jane—Joan Burroughs, Dean—Neal Cassady, Carlo Marx—Allen Ginsberg.

2. An entry about James Wideman Lee by C. C. Pearson appears in the *Dictionary of American Biography,* 1933 ed. Information about him can also be found in Ray Eldon Heibert, *Courtier to the Crowd: The Story of Ivy Lee and the Development of Public Relations* (Ames: Iowa State University Press, 1966), pp. 16–19. Information on William S. Burroughs can be found in the *DAB,* 1944 Supplement, entry by Charles O. Paullin.

3. Heibert, *Courtier,* p. 72.

4. Upton Sinclair, "Poison Ivy," in *The Brass Check* (Pasadena, Calif.: the author, 1920), pp. 311–13.

5. David Sanders, "John Dos Passos," in *Writers at Work: The Paris Review Interviews,* 4th series, ed. George Plimpton and Wilfrid Sheed (New York: Viking, 1976), pp. 77–78.

6. Information about Ivy Lee is drawn from Heibert, *Courtier.*

7. Conrad Knickerbocker, "William Burroughs," in *Writers at Work: The Paris Review Interviews,* 3d series, ed. George Plimpton (New York, 1967), p. 160.

8. Ibid. p. 174.

9. Information in this paragraph is drawn from an interview with the author, 4 April 1980.

10. Victor Bockris, *With William Burroughs* (New York, 1981), p. xiv.

11. *Cobble Stone Gardens* (New York, 1976).

12. "Life With Father," *Esquire,* September 1971, p. 115.

13. A comment repeated in several interviews: Nina Sutton, "In Search of the Connection," *Guardian,* 5 July 1964, p. 7; Daniel Odier, *The Job* (New York, 1970), p. 116; Philippe Mikriamos, *William S. Burroughs* (Paris: Seghers, 1975), pp. 147–48; Laura Delp, "Inside the William Burroughs Bunker," *Weekly Soho News,* 24–30 March 1977, p. 8. During the late 1960s and early 1970s when Burroughs was drawing upon childhood memories in his fiction, misogynistic themes were most prominent in his work, as shown in *The Job* (1969), *The Wild Boys* (1971), and *Exterminator!* (1973). In fact, *The Wild Boys* can be seen as a mythic boys' rebellion against their mothers and an escape to an all-boy paradise of bodily pleasures. Barry Miles remarked in Bockris's *With William Burroughs* that Burroughs attempted to create an all-male society for himself in London during this period (p. 47).

14. John Tytell, *Naked Angels: The Lives and Literature of the Beat Generation* (New York, 1976), p. 37.

15. Miles Associates, *A Descriptive Catalogue of the William S. Burroughs Archive* (London, 1973), pp. 74–80.

16. In *The Yage Letters* Burroughs says, "In the U.S. you have to be a deviant or exist in dreary boredom. Even a man like Oppenheimer is a deviant tolerated for his usefulness. Make no mistake *all* intellectuals are deviants in the U.S." Written with Allen Ginsberg (San Francisco, 1963), p. 41.

17. Burroughs refers to his college years in the preface to *Junkie* and in interviews with Knickerbocker and John Tytell, "An Interview with William S. Burroughs," in *The Beat Diary,* the unspeakable visions of the individual series, no. 5, ed. Arthur and Kit Knight (California, Pa., 1977).

18. While in Europe in 1937, Burroughs married Ilse Herzfeld Klapper, a German Jew seeking to escape the Nazi regime. They were divorced in 1946. Burroughs refers to this marriage in the Tytell interview in *Beat Diary,* p. 43, and in Bockris, *With Burroughs,* p. 41.

19. Tytell, *Naked Angels,* p. 38; "A Literary Autobiography," p. 75.

20. *Nova Express* (New York, 1964), pp. 127–32.

21. Burroughs remarked in the Delp interview that the rejection of the *Titanic* piece discouraged his writing ambitions for some time.

22. "The White Negro," a seminal essay of the 1950s, was first published in *Dissent* 4 (Summer 1957):276–93. It has been reprinted in Mailer's *Advertisements for Myself* (New York: Putnam's, 1959), pp. 311–31, and as a monograph by City Lights Books (San Francisco).

23. Mailer, "The White Negro," in *Advertisements,* p. 322.

24. Ibid. p. 328.

25. Bruce Cook, *The Beat Generation* (New York, 1971), p. 94.

26. *Junkie* (New York: Ace Books, 1964), p. 125.

27. Ann Charters says in *Kerouac: A Biography* (New York, 1974), p. 387, that Huncke was the source of the term "beat" for Ginsberg and Kerouac, who later applied the word to their generation. Burroughs, however, uses the term "hip" or "hipster" in *Junkie.* Huncke's relationship with Burroughs, Ginsberg, and Kerouac is discussed in Charters's biography of Kerouac, in Tytell's *Naked Angels,* and in Tytell's interview with Burroughs in *Beat Diary.* (Charters's biography was first published in hardcover by Straight Arrow Books [San Francisco, 1973], but the Warner paperback edition cited here is more readily available and contains revisions that correct earlier inaccuracies.)

28. Knickerbocker, "William Burroughs," p. 162. What Burroughs calls "the carny world" has been discussed as "the sporting life" by sociologist Ned Polsky in *Hustlers, Beats, and Others* (New York: Anchor Books, 1969), pp. 18–24.

29. See Charters, *Kerouac,* p. 56.

30. John Tytell, "A Conversation with Allen Ginsberg," *Partisan Review* 41 (1974):254.

31. Burroughs appears as a character in the following novels by Kerouac: *The Town and the City, On the Road, The Subterraneans, Doctor Sax, Book of Dreams, Desolation Angels, Vanity of Duluoz*. See appendix 4 to Ann Charters's *Kerouac*.

32. Charters, *Kerouac*, p. 56; Tytell, Burroughs interview, p. 39; Tytell, Ginsberg interview, p. 254.

33. See Gerard Malanga, "An Interview with William Burroughs," in *The Beat Book*, the unspeakable visions of the individual series, no. 4, ed. Arthur and Glee Knight (California, Pa., 1974), p. 91; and the Tytell interview in *Beat Diary*, pp. 36–37.

34. This collaboration is discussed in Charters, *Kerouac*, p. 57, in the Tytell interview in *Beat Diary*, p. 39, and in the *Paris Review* interview with Kerouac by Ted Berrigan in *Writers at Work: The Paris Review Interviews*, 4th series, ed. George Plimpton and Wilfrid Sheed (New York: Viking, 1976), p. 371. The murder of Dave Kammerer by Lucien Carr made the front page of the *New York Times* on August 17, 1944. There were seven followup stories. Carr claimed that Kammerer, a known homosexual, had attacked him and that Carr had stabbed Kammerer in self-defense. Carr was eventually sentenced to several years in prison. The murderer and the victim were friends of Burroughs's from St. Louis and had become acquainted with Kerouac and Ginsberg. Both Burroughs and Kerouac were indicted as material witnesses.

35. Ginsberg narrates the story of the manuscript in his introduction to the new Penguin edition of the novel: *Junky* (New York, 1977), pp. v–ix. (This edition revises the spelling of the title.)

36. See Berrigan's interview with Kerouac in *Writers at Work*, p. 371; Charters, *Kerouac*, pp. 284, 395; the Tytell interview in *Beat Diary*, p. 37; the Malanga interview in *The Beat Book*, p. 91; and Burroughs's introduction to *Naked Lunch* (New York, 1962), p. v.

37. Knickerbocker, "William Burroughs," p. 145.

38. These years are chronicled in *Junkie*. Burroughs refers to some of these events in the Knickerbocker and Tytell interviews. Also see Charters, *Kerouac*, pp. 85, 104–5, 118–21, 153–61, 384.

39. According to legend, Burroughs accidentally killed his wife while trying to shoot a champagne glass off the top of her head, William Tell style. In the Knickerbocker interview, p. 167, he denied this story; in Bockris's *With Burroughs*, p. 44, he confirmed it. Howard Brookner's film biography, *Burroughs*, made with Burrough's cooperation, reports the William Tell story.

40. See his comments on dreams in the Knickerbocker interview, p. 149; Odier, *The Job*, p. 95, 188, 166–68; the Malanga interview, p. 94; the Tytell interview in *Beat Diary*, p. 43; in "William Burroughs," interview by Robert Palmer, *Rolling Stone*, 11 May 1972, p. 51; and in "Beat Godfather meets Glitter Mainman," interview by Craig Capetas and David Bowie, *Rolling Stone*, 28 February 1974, p. 26.

41. Charters, *Kerouac*, pp. 154–55, 384.

42. "Letter from a Master Addict to Dangerous Drugs," *British Journal of*

Addiction 53 (January 1957):119–31; rpt. in the Grove Press edition of *Naked Lunch* as an appendix.

43. "Points of Distinction between Sedative and Consciousness-expanding Drugs," *Evergreen Review,* no. 34 (December 1964):72–74.

44. Knickerbocker, "William Burroughs," pp. 146, 150.

45. Odier, *The Job,* p. 153.

46. Burroughs discusses the composition of *Naked Lunch* and the following novels from one thousand pages of manuscript in the Palmer interview, p. 52; the Malanga interview, p. 109; and the Tytell interview in *Beat Diary,* pp. 37, 42.

47. Odier, *The Job,* p. 139. Burroughs's most important discussions of Dr. Dent and the apomorphine treatment appear in the introduction to *Naked Lunch*; in "Kicking Drugs: A Very Personal Story," *Harper's,* July 1967, pp. 39–42; in the Knickerbocker interview, p. 147; and in Odier, *The Job,* pp. 139–52. Readers may also refer to John Yerbury Dent's *Anxiety and Its Treatment* (London: John Murray, 1941). The publication of Burrough's *Letters to Allen Ginsberg, 1953– 1957* (New York, 1982) somewhat revises Burrough's statement to Odier, for the letters show, as Burroughs himself admits in the preface, that a great deal of *Naked Lunch* was written while Burroughs was an addict. The dramatic reversal attributed to apomorphine is another example of biography transformed into legend.

48. Bockris, *With Burroughs,* p. 24; descriptions of Burroughs at work on *Naked Lunch* are provided in Jack Kerouac's *Desolation Angels* (New York: Putnam's, 1965), pp. 310–11; Paul Bowles's "Burroughs in Tangier," *Big Table,* no. 2 (Summer 1959):42–43, and Alan Ansen's "Anyone Who Can Pick Up a Frying Pan Owns Death," *Big Table,* no. 2 (Summer 1959):pp. 32–41.

49. Bockris, *With Burroughs,* p. 26.

50. Author's interview with John Calder, 9 May 1981.

51. "Ugh," *Times Literary Supplement,* 14 November 1963, p. 947, correspondence weekly until 23 January 1964.

52. Paul Bowles, *Without Stopping* (New York, 1972), p. 349. Kerouac was similarly unimpressed with his 1961 psilocybin experience under Leary's guidance, remarking that "Walking on water wasn't built in a day." See Dennis McNally, *Desolate Angel* (New York, 1979), p. 293.

53. Bockris, *With Burroughs,* p. 70.

54. Odier, *The Job*; Philippe Mikriamos, *William S. Burroughs* (Paris: Seghers, 1975), the first critical book on Burroughs in French. Burroughs's translator and critic, Gérard-Georges Lemaire, organized the Colloque de Tanger in Geneva, Switzerland, a conference in honor of Burroughs and Gysin; some of the proceedings were published in *Colloque de Tanger* (Paris: Bourgois, 1976). Lemaire also contributed a critical essay to *Oeuvre croisée,* trans. Lemaire and C. Taylor (Paris, 1976), published in English as *The Third Mind* (New York, 1978). Serge Grunberg's *A la recherche d'un corps: Langage et silence dans l'oeuvre de William S. Burroughs* was published in 1979 (Paris: Seuil). Publications also continued by Burroughs's translators and collaborators Mary Beach and Claude Pélieu.

55. Bockris, *With Burroughs,* p. 74.

56. See Tytell, *Naked Angels,* p. 135; Cook, *Beat Generation,* p. 179; the Jeff Shero interviews in *Rat,* 4–14 October 1968, pp. 1, 10–11; 18–31 October 1968, p. 10; 13 December–2 January 1968/69, pp. 5, 14.

57. Interview with the author, 4 April 1980.

58. Capetas and Bowie, "Beat Godfather," p. 26.

59. Cook, *Beat Generation,* pp. 165, 184.

60. Portions of Mottram's book were first published in *Intrepid,* nos. 14/15 (Fall/Winter 1969/70), ed. Allen de Loach. De Loach published the complete monograph in 1971 (Buffalo, N.Y., Beau Fleuve Series, no. 2). The 1977 London edition is revised and updated.

61. Although Burroughs has never mentioned the influence of Whitman on his work, Whitman's influence upon Ginsberg, Burroughs's friend and collaborator, is pervasive and repeatedly acknowledged.

Chapter Two

1. See Allen Ginsberg's introduction to the Penguin edition of *Junky* (New York, 1977), pp. v–x.

2. The Penguin edition publishes the complete, original text.

3. "Publisher's Note," in *Junkie* (New York: Ace Books, 1964), p. 2.

4. Introduction to *Junky,* p. ix.

5. Knickerbocker, p. 145.

6. *Junkie* (New York: Ace Books, 1964). Page references in the text are from this edition.

7. See Odier, *The Job,* p. 23.

8. See Gordon Ball, "Reader's Guide," in Allen Ginsberg, *Journals: Early Fifties-Early Sixties* (New York: Grove, 1977), p. xvii; and authors' acknowledgment, William Burroughs and Allen Ginsberg, *The Yage Letters* (San Francisco, 1963), p. 2.

9. Ansen, "Anyone Who Can," pp. 32–41; and Robert Creeley, "A New Testament," *Outburst,* no. 1 (1961):n. p.

10. "In Quest of Yage," *Big Table,* no. 2 (Summer 1959): pp. 44–65.

11. William Burroughs and Allen Ginsberg, *The Yage Letters* (San Francisco, 1963). Page references in the text are from this edition.

12. The doctor's book about his treatment for addiction is also relevant to Burroughs's fiction: Dent, *Anxiety and Its Treatment.*

13. "Deposition: Testimony Concerning a Sickness," *Evergreen Review,* no. 11 (January–February 1960):15–23. This essay was later included in the Grove Press edition of *Naked Lunch.*

14. "Kicking Drugs," pp. 39–42.

15. Ibid., p. 41.

16. Odier, *The Job,* p. 139.

17. Michael Barry Goodman, *Contemporary Literary Censorship: The Case History of Burroughs' Naked Lunch* (Metuchen, N.J.: Scarecrow, 1981), p. 249.

18. The legal history that follows is drawn from Felice Flanery Lewis, *Literature, Obscenity, and the Law* (Carbondale: Southern Illinois University Press, 1976), pp. 188–225, and from Goodman, *Censorship.*

19. The text of the Massachusetts Supreme Court's ruling is part of the prefatory material in Grove's Evergreen Black Cat Edition of *Naked Lunch* (New York, 1966), pp. viii–ix.

20. William S. Burroughs, *Naked Lunch* (New York, 1962). Page references in the text are from this edition. Pagination of the Grove Press hardcover and paperback editions of *Naked Lunch* is identical except for prefatory material.

21. Knickerbocker, "William Burroughs," p. 171.

22. Mottram, *William Burroughs,* p. 57.

23. Ann Morrisette, "An Account of the Events Preceding the Death of Bill Burroughs," *Evergreen Review,* no. 29 (March–April 1963):107.

24. Burroughs's work can be compared to the pop art of Andy Warhol, Roy Lichtenstein, Jim Dine, George Segal, Claes Oldenburg, James Rosenquist, Robert Rauschenberg, and Richard Hamilton, whose work is contemporary with his fiction.

25. Mary McCarthy, "Burroughs' *Naked Lunch,*" in *The Writing on the Wall and Other Essays* (New York, 1971), p. 168.

26. An oft-repeated statement first published in a Grove Press publicity pamphlet in 1962, documented by Goodman, *Censorship,* p. 160.

27. McCarthy's "Burroughs' *Naked Lunch*" was first published in *Encounter* 20 (April 1963):92–98; rpt. *New York Review of Books* 1, no. 1 (1963):4–5; rpt. *Writing on the Wall,* pp. 42–53.

28. "The Great Burroughs Affair," *New Republic,* 1 December 1962, pp. 21–23, correspondence weekly through 2 January 1963; "The New Immoralists," *Commentary* 39 (April 1965):66–69; correspondence followed in the next issue; *Times Literary Supplement,* 21 November 1963, p. 947, correspondence weekly through 23 January 1964; "Whither Ugh," 30 January 1964, p. 87. The "Ugh" reviewer discussed several other books by Burroughs in addition to *Naked Lunch.*

Chapter Three

1. Burroughs also compiled *Dead Fingers Talk* (London, 1963), a novel that incorporates routines from *Naked Lunch* and the other three novels in order to introduce his work to the British public. *Dead Fingers Talk* is not discussed in this chapter because it contains so little new material and because it has not been published in the United States.

2. Palmer, "William Burroughs," p. 52.

3. In the Palmer interview, p. 52, Burroughs carefully points out that the use of the cutup technique separates the trilogy from *Naked Lunch* and gives the three later novels a formal unity. In *The Job,* p. 13, he also separates *Naked Lunch* from the following novels on the basis of the cutup technique.

4. See Robin Lydenberg, "Cut-Up: Negative Poetics in William Burroughs and Roland Barthes," *Comparative Literature Studies* 15 (1978):414–30; and Gérard-Georges Lemaire, "23 Stitches Taken," in *The Third Mind*, by William S. Burroughs and Brion Gysin, pp. 9–24.

5. Burroughs has used this term many times to describe his work. The earliest reference is in Pierre Dommergues, "Rencontre avec William Burroughs," *Les Langues Modernes* 59 (January–February 1965): 79–83. This interview is actually a translation of part of the transcript of an interview Eric Mottram conducted with Burroughs for the BBC in 1965.

6. Burroughs had begun reading Reich in the 1930s, kept up with his work, and owned an orgone box. "Emotional plague," "regulation," and "immunization" are Reichian terms that are echoed in Burroughs's work. Reich's discussion of the emotional plague in *Character Analysis* is relevant to Burroughs: "It [the emotional plague] made an inroad into human society with the mass suppression of genital sexuality; it became an endemic disease which has been tormenting people the world over for thousands of years. There are no grounds for assuming that the emotional plague is passed on from mother to child in a hereditary way. According to our knowledge, it is an endemic illness, like schizophrenia or cancer, with one notable difference, i.e., it is essentially manifested in *social life*." Wilhelm Reich, *Character Analysis*, tr. Vincent Carfagno, 3d ed. (New York: Farrar, Strauss & Giroux, 1972), p. 504. Reich's *The Invasion of Compulsory Sex-Morality* (1931) and *The Mass Psychology of Fascism* (1933) are also relevant to Burroughs's work.

7. *The Ticket That Exploded* (New York, 1967). Page references in the text are from this edition.

8. "The Invisible Generation" was first published in two parts in *International Times*, 14 November 1966, p. 6, and 16 January 1967, p. 6.

9. Burroughs acknowledges the paradox of fighting the control of words with words in the Knickerbocker interview, p. 154.

10. The same words are applied to apomorphine in "Kicking Drugs," p. 41.

11. The American Grove Press editions of *The Ticket That Exploded* and *The Soft Machine* are different from the original Paris Olympia Press editions. There are omissions and additions, different typography.

12. Burroughs's most detailed discussion of Scientology appears in *The Job*, pp. 24–39.

13. The parallels between Burroughs's thinking about language in the trilogy and Roland Barthes's structuralist analysis in *Mythologies* and Barthes's other work of the 1950s and early 1960s are striking. Although Burroughs was living in Paris during this period, he has never mentioned any direct contact with structuralist theorists. He seems to have arrived at similar conclusions independently, perhaps through his own anthropological studies. At any rate, Burroughs's mode of thought is always metaphorical and expressed in artistic form, making it difficult to transpose his concepts into abstract, theoretical arguments and critique them as such.

14. Eric Mottram, *William Burroughs: the Algebra of Need* (London, 1977), p. 102.

15. Compare Claude Lévi-Strauss, "Structural Study of Myth," *Journal of American Folklore* 68 (1955):428–43.

16. *Nova Express* (New York, 1964). Page numbers in the text are from this edition.

17. Called "the first great cutup collage" by Burroughs in the Knickerbocker interview, p. 153.

18. This satirical fantasy is the piece Burroughs wrote with Kells Elvins in 1938. Its inclusion here is typical of Burroughs's mixture of old and new material and his desire to create a unified body of work.

19. Burroughs told Knickerbocker, "I do definitely mean what I say to be taken literally, yes, to make people aware of the true criminality of our times, to wise up the marks. All of my work is directed against those who are bent, through stupidity or design, on blowing up the planet or rendering it uninhabitable" (p. 174).

20. Mottram, for example, calls Burroughs an elitist who rejects all group action in favor of individual anarchic subversion (*William Burroughs,* pp. 112–13).

21. See Burroughs's comments on the similarities between the United States and the Soviet Union in the Knickerbocker interview, p. 173.

22. Céline set a precedent for this style of punctuation, and Burroughs is one of his admirers.

23. Burroughs has repeated this statement in different forms many times over the years. The first published appearance is probably "The Cut-Up Method of Brion Gysin," *A Casebook on the Beat,* ed. Thomas Parkinson (New York: Crowell, 1961), pp. 105–6. See also Odier, *The Job,* p. 13; *The Third Mind,* p. 34; and Bockris, *With Burroughs,* p. 6.

24. "Artwork" is my own coinage to express the idea of process and to contrast with the concept of a work of art as a finished product.

25. "Censorship," *Transatlantic Review,* No. 11 (Winter 1962): p. 6.

26. Malanga interview, p. 94.

27. Joan Didion, "Wired for Shock Treatments," *Book Week,* 27 March 1966, pp. 2–3; Theodore Solotaroff, "The Algebra of Need," *New Republic,* 5 August 1967, pp. 29–34; Terry Southern, "Rolling Over our Nerve-endings," *Book Week,* 8 November 1964, pp. 5, 31.

Chapter Four

1. Daniel Odier, *Entretiens avec William Burroughs* (Paris, 1969), tr. *The Job,* revised and enlarged (New York, 1970).

2. Robert Palmer, "William Burroughs," *Rolling Stone,* 11 May 1972, p. 52; hereafter cited in the text as RP.

3. *The Retreat Diaries* (New York, 1976), n.p. "Trungpa" refers to Chog-

yam Trungpa, founder of the Naropa Institute in Boulder, Colorado, and Allen Ginsberg's spiritual advisor. He is a Tibetan Buddhist.

4. *Cities of the Red Night* (New York, 1981), p. xviii.

5. Burroughs notes in *Ports of Saints* (Berkeley, 1980) that "dreams in males are accompanied by erection even though the content of the dream is non-sexual" (p. 165).

6. *The Wild Boys* (New York, 1971). Page references in the text are from this edition.

7. Interview with the author.

8. *Exterminator!* (New York, 1973). Page references in the text are from this edition.

9. *Exterminator!* includes a new routine with this title.

10. Interview with the author. Forsyth is the author of the best-selling thrillers *Day of the Jackal, The Dogs of War*, and others.

11. The B-23 virus continues Burroughs's use of the number 23 as a recurrent motif in his work. Although Mottram suggests (p. 261) that the number derives from the number of chromosomes, Burroughs told the author that it was an arbitrary fixation with no special source or meaning: "It's just a number I observed turning up again and again. As soon as you start paying attention to a number, then you'll see it. If I see anything with the number 23, it catches my attention."

12. *Cities of the Red Night*, p. 332.

13. *The Retreat Diaries*, n.p.

14. Hendin, untitled review, *Saturday Review*, 30 October 1971, pp. 46, 49–50; Kazin, untitled review, *New York Times Book Review*, 12 December 1981, pp. 4, 22–23.

15. *Naked Angels*, p. 138. Tytell is one of the few academic critics who discuss the fiction written after *Nova Express*.

16. Thomas M. Disch, "Pleasures of Hanging," *New York Times Book Review*, 15 March 1981, p. 15.

17. See Anthony Burgess, "Burroughs's Bad Dreams," *Saturday Review*, March 1981, p. 66; Julia M. Klein, untitled review, *New Republic*, 18 April 1981, pp. 39–40.

18. *Port of Saints* had not been widely reviewed in the United States at the time this study was completed.

Chapter Five

1. Some critics have taken Burroughs's work more seriously and have viewed the works as a series. See essays by Hassan, Hendin, Mottram, Nelson, Skerl, Tanner, Tytell, and Vernon listed in the bibliography. These critics place a high value upon the modern novel as an avant-garde art form.

2. Richard Pearce uses this term to describe Burroughs's comic technique

in *Stages of the Clown: Perspectives on Modern Fiction from Dostoevsky to Beckett* (Carbondale, Ill., 1970), pp. 88–94.

3. This definition of the avant-garde is drawn from Renato Poggioli, *The Theory of the Avant-Garde* (Cambridge: Harvard University Press, 1968).

4. Allen Ginsberg, for example, received the National Book Award for his *Fall of America* (San Francisco: City Lights, 1972).

Selected Bibliography

Because of the nature of Burroughs's artwork as defined in this text, it is impossible to select the most important short pieces that have appeared in periodicals over the years. Furthermore, most of Burroughs's periodical appearances have been in little magazines and underground journals that are difficult to locate. Burroughs usually selects his best pieces—both fiction and nonfiction—for inclusion in his books, and a complete list of these follows. Also listed are interviews containing important biographical and theoretical statements by Burroughs himself. A chronological listing of primary materials reflects Burroughs's artistic process and publication history better than the conventional alphabetical catalog. Readers interested in Burroughs's periodical publications should consult the detailed bibliographies listed below.

PRIMARY SOURCES

1. Novels (arranged chronologically)

Original publication is given first, if not in the United States, followed by first publication in the United States, then first publication in England. Entries conclude with the currently available reprint, if any is available.

Junkie. By "William Lee," with *Narcotic Agent* by Maurice Helbrant. New York: Ace Books (paperback), 1953; London: Digit Books (paperback), 1957. *Junkie.* By William Burroughs. Foreword by Carl Solomon. New York: Ace Books (paperback), 1964. *Junky.* The complete original text (with revised spelling of title). Introduction by Allen Ginsberg. New York: Penguin (paperback), 1977.

The Naked Lunch. Paris: Olympia, 1959. *Naked Lunch.* New York: Grove, 1962. With "Deposition: Testimony Concerning a Sickness" as introduction and "Letter from a Master Addict to Dangerous Drugs" as appendix. London: Calder, 1964. Reprint edition, with preface, *"Naked Lunch* on Trial" (excerpts of trial testimony): New York: Grove (First Evergreen Black Cat Edition, paperback), 1966.

The Soft Machine. Paris: Olympia Press, 1961. Revised edition, New York: Grove, 1966; London: Calder & Boyars, 1968. Reprint editions: New York: Grove (First Evergreen Black Cat Edition, paperback), 1967; included in *Three Novels,* New York: Grove (paperback), 1981.

The Ticket That Exploded. Paris: Olympia, 1962. Revised edition, New York: Grove, 1967; London: Calder & Boyars, 1968. Reprint edition: New York:

Grove (First Evergreen Black Cat Edition, paperback), 1968.

Dead Fingers Talk. London: John Calder, 1963.

Nova Express. New York: Grove, 1964; London: Jonathan Cape, 1966. Reprint editions: New York: Grove (First Evergreen Black Cat Edition, paperback), 1965; included in *Three Novels,* New York: Grove (paperback), 1981.

The Wild Boys. New York: Grove, 1971; London: Calder & Boyars, 1972. Reprint edition: *Three Novels.* New York: Grove (paperback), 1981.

Exterminator! New York: Viking, 1973. Reprint edition: New York: Penguin (paperback), 1979.

Port of Saints. London: Covent Garden, 1975. Revised edition, Berkeley: Blue Wind, 1980.

Cities of the Red Night. New York: Holt, Rinehart & Winston, 1981; London: Calder, 1981. Reprint edition: New York: Holt, Rinehart & Winston (paperback), 1982.

2. Other books and pamphlets (arranged chronologically)

First publication is followed by the currently available reprint, if any. Brief annotations indicate contents.

Minutes To Go. With Sinclair Beiles, Gregory Corso, and Brion Gysin. Paris: Two Cities, 1960. First cutup experiments by the four authors. Burroughs contributes several short prose pieces and poems made up of his own texts, those of other writers, and newspaper articles.

The Exterminator. With Brion Gysin. San Francisco: Auerhahn (paperback), 1960. First cutup experiments by the two authors. Burroughs's contribution consists of several short prose pieces using his own writing, other writers, and newspaper texts. Several permutation poems and calligraphic drawings by Gysin are included.

The Yage Letters. With Allen Ginsberg. San Francisco: City Lights (paperback), 1963. Includes "In Search of Yage," a short epistolary novel by Burroughs, written in 1953; "Seven Years Later," consisting of a letter by Ginsberg to Burroughs and Burroughs's reply, written in 1960; and "Epilogue," consisting of a letter to the reader by Ginsberg and a cutup by Burroughs, written in 1963.

Roosevelt After Inauguration. New York: Fuck You Press (pamphlet), 1964. Burroughs's first routine (a short satirical fantasy), originally part of "In Search of Yage."

Health Bulletin: APO-33, A Metabolic Regulator. New York: Fuck You Press (pamphlet), 1965. A cutup piece on the subject of apomorphine and the Nova conspiracy.

Time. With drawings by Brion Gysin. New York: 'C' Press (pamphlet), 1965. A cutup parody of *Time* magazine, emphasizing the themes of time, death, and control.

Valentine's Day Reading. New York: American Theatre for Poets (pamphlet), 1965. Two short fictions about Dutch Schultz and Bradly Martin.

So Who Owns Death TV? With Claude Pélieu and Carl Weissner. San Francisco: Beach Books (pamphlet), 1967. A collaborative cutup fiction.

The Dead Star. San Francisco: Nova Broadcast Press (broadside), 1969. A fold-out broadside in newspaper-column format; text a cutup on the death of Dutch Schultz.

The Last Words of Dutch Schultz, A Fiction in the Form of a Film Script. London: Cape Goliard, 1970. Reprint edition: New York: Seaver Books (paperback), 1981. A montage on the subject of Dutch Schultz's life and death in the form of a film script with photographs.

Ali's Smile. London: Unicorn, 1971. A short novel using Moroccan and London imagery, accompanied by a record of Burroughs reading a draft of the text.

Electronic Revolution. Cambridge, England: Blackmoor Head, 1971. Combined essay and fiction on the use of tape cutups to destroy sociolinguistic control systems.

Brion Gysin Let the Mice In. West Glover, Vt.: Something Else Press, 1973. Texts of cutups and multimedia experiments by Burroughs, Brion Gysin, and Ian Sommerville. Consists of several short pieces previously published in periodicals in the 1960s.

Mayfair Academy Series More or Less. Brighton, Sussex: Urgency Press Rip-Off (pamphlet), 1973. Short fiction previously published in periodicals from 1968 to 1973 with two additional pieces by Roy Pennington.

White Subway. London: Aloes seolA (paperback), 1973. A collection of short cutup pieces previously published in periodicals in the 1960s, ending with reprints of "Anyone Who Can Pick Up a Frying Pan Owns Death" by Alan Ansen and "Burroughs in Tangier" by Paul Bowles.

The Book of Breeething. Illustrations by Robert F. Gale. Berkeley: Blue Wind, 1975. 2d ed., 1980. Words and pictures illustrate linguistic controls and ways to evade them, with hieroglyphics and Hassan i Sabbah's assassin cult as models.

Cobble Stone Gardens. Cherry Valley, N.Y.: Cherry Valley Editions, 1976. Dedicated to Burroughs's parents, a fictionalized memoir and prose poem about his parents, his youth, St. Louis, time, and death, juxtaposed with routines from *Naked Lunch* and *Wild Boys* material.

Oeuvre croisée. Translated into French by Gérard-Georges Lemaire and C. Taylor. Paris: Flammarion, 1976. Published in English as *The Third Mind*. With Brion Gysin. New York: Viking, 1978. Reprint edition. New York: Seaver Books (paperback), 1982. A collection of essays, fiction, poems, and drawings written from 1960 to 1973 illustrating the authors' theory of the cutup. Includes a critical essay by Gérard-Georges Lemaire.

The Retreat Diaries. Introduction by James Grauerholz. New York: City Moon, 1976. A montage of dreams recorded over a two-week period while on a retreat at a Buddhist center in Vermont in 1975, with an explanatory essay by Burroughs. Concludes with "A Dream of Tibet" by Allen Ginsberg (1960) and a dream recorded by James Grauerholz in 1974.

Ah Pook is Here and Other Texts. London: Calder, 1979. Contains three fictions: "Ah Pook is Here," a new piece, a Mayan fantasy about controlling death; and two previously published pieces, "The Book of Breeething" and "Electronic Revolution."

Blade Runner: A Movie. Berkeley: Blue Wind, 1979. A short novel: a satirical fantasy about the decline of New York City and the American health-care system.

Dr. Benway. Santa Barbara: Bradford Morrow, 1979. A variant passage of the "Benway" section of *Naked Lunch* with a new introduction by Burroughs.

Where Naked Troubadours Shoot Snotty Baboons. Northridge, Calif.: Lord John Press (broadside), 1979. Excerpt from *Cities of the Red Night.*

Roosevelt After Inauguration. San Francisco: City Lights (paperback), 1979. Four routines, all on political themes, including Burroughs's first routine (title piece, 1953) and three from the 1970s.

Early Routines. Santa Barbara: Cadmus, 1981. Previously unpublished routines from the 1950s. Style and themes parallel *Naked Lunch.*

Letters to Allen Ginsberg, 1953–1957. New York: Full Court, 1982. Burroughs's letters to Ginsberg (and a few to others) during his residence in Tangier, chronicling his personal life and the composition of *Naked Lunch.*

3. Selected interviews (arranged chronologically)

Corso, Gregory, and Ginsberg, Allen. "Interview with William Burroughs." *Journal for the Protection of All Beings,* no. 1 (San Francisco: City Lights, 1961):79–83. Burroughs's first published interview in which he assumes the voice and persona of "Agent Lee" in discussing major themes in his current fiction: political control systems, the Nova conspiracy, cutups, a mutation in consciousness, silence, and apocalypse.

Knickerbocker, Conrad. "William Burroughs." In *Writers at Work: The Paris Review Interviews.* Edited by Alfred Kazin. New York: Viking, 1967, pp. 143–74. Burroughs's most widely known interview, conducted soon after the trilogy was completed (1965). Discusses themes and techniques in his first four novels, in effect explicating his mythological world and its relation to his use of montage and cutups. Major topics: drugs, cutups, the carny world, the Nova conspiracy, pseudoscience, alteration of consciousness. Important biographical material is also included.

Odier, Daniel. *Entretiens avec William Burroughs.* Paris: Editions Pierre Belfond, 1969. Translated as *The Job,* revised and enlarged. New York: Grove, 1970; London: Jonathan Cape, 1970. *The Job,* further enlarged. New York: Grove, 1974. A series of interviews with Odier became a book-length collaboration as Burroughs added essays and short fiction to illustrate his thinking about drugs, sexuality and women, cutups, hieroglyphics, the family and the nation-state, censorship, time and death, achieving autonomy, and his multimedia experiments of the 1960s. Shows Burroughs moving from the Nova conspiracy to the wild boys as a primary metaphor.

Sutton, Nina. "In Search of the Connection." *Manchester Guardian,* 5 July 1969, p. 7. Good illustration of Burroughs's transition from *Nova Express* to *The Wild Boys,* containing informative summations of his views on drugs, cut-ups, the novel form, sexuality, misogyny, sociolinguistic control systems, and the political protests of the 1960s.

Palmer, Robert. "William Burroughs." *Rolling Stone,* 11 May 1972, pp. 48–53. Interview with Burroughs and Gysin conducted soon after the publication of *The Wild Boys.* Important discussion of theory, techniques, and themes that distinguish Burroughs's earlier and later group of novels. Major topics: art as action, the importance of the text, the youth revolt, and collaborations with Gysin.

Malanga, Gerard. "An Interview with William Burroughs." *The Beat Book.* Edited by Arthur and Glee Knight. California, Pa.: the unspeakable visions of the individual series, 1974, pp. 90–112. Conducted soon after Burroughs's return to the United States (1974). Major topics: the creation and publication of several works, friendships with other writers, Burroughs's reading, the sources of his writing in dreams, and the "one book" that is his art.

Tytell, John. "An Interview with William Burroughs." *The Beat Diary.* Edited by Arthur and Kit Knight. California, Pa.: the unspeakable visions of the individual series, 1977, pp. 35–49. Conducted in 1974, provides Burroughs's most extended discussion of biography and chronology.

Bockris, Victor. *With William Burroughs: A Report from the Bunker.* New York: Seaver, 1981. Conversations between Burroughs and his acquaintances from 1974 to 1980, recorded by a journalist and professional interviewer. Selected excerpts organized topically and geographically. A valuable book for the biographical information contributed by friends and for the portrait that emerges of Burroughs, the private man, in his sixties.

Skerl, Jennie. "An Interview with William S. Burroughs." *Modern Language Studies* 12 (Summer 1982):3–17. A recent interview (1980) in which Burroughs discusses his life since his return to the United States, his recent fiction, his current theories of art and writing, his current reading, and some biographical background.

SECONDARY SOURCES

Secondary sources include all works in English published in the United States and Great Britain. Readers interested in foreign-language criticism of Burroughs should consult the bibliographies listed as well as the annual bibliography of the Modern Language Association.

List of abbreviations used in annotations:

E: *Exterminator!*
J: *Junkie*
NE: *Nova Express*
NL: *Naked Lunch*
SM: *The Soft Machine*
TE: *The Exterminator*
TTE: *The Ticket That Exploded*
WB: *The Wild Boys*
YL: *The Yage Letters*

1. Bibliographies

Goodman, Michael B. *William S. Burroughs: An Annotated Bibliography of His Works and Criticism.* New York: Garland, 1975. A critical bibliography of works, biographical articles, and criticism, alphabetically listed; and a chronological list of letters and other papers held at Columbia and Syracuse University libraries. Especially valuable for its annotations of unpublished materials and diverse secondary sources.

Maynard, Joe, and Miles, Barry. *William S. Burroughs: A Bibliography, 1953–73.* Charlottesville: University of Virginia, 1978. A comprehensive and accurate analytical bibliography of Burroughs's works, in chronological order up to 1973, and including publications in all countries. Includes books; pamphlets; contributions to books, anthologies, and periodicals; foreign editions; interviews; records and tapes. An invaluable resource and the best illustration of Burroughs's lifelong artwork on three continents.

Miles Associates. *A Descriptive Catalogue of the William S. Burroughs Archive.* London: Covent Garden, 1973. A list of the collection of manuscripts, correspondence, and other papers by Burroughs and Gysin at the International Center of Art and Communication in Vaduz, Liechtenstein, indicating the contents of the collection but providing limited information. Includes Burroughs's "Literary Autobiography."

Skerl, Jennie. "A William S. Burroughs Bibliography." *Serif* 11 (Summer 1974):12–20. A chronological checklist of Burroughs's works in all media, and an alphabetical list of criticism from a variety of sources. The organization of entries is useful for the critic.

2. Books

Goodman, Michael Barry. *Contemporary Literary Censorship: The Case History of Burroughs' Naked Lunch.* Metuchen, N.J.: Scarecrow, 1981. A narrative history of the writing, publication, critical reception, and censorship of *Naked Lunch* in the United States: "the last work of literature to be censored by the academy, the U.S. Post Office, the U.S. Customs Service, and state and local government." A valuable source of much previously unpublished material.

Mottram, Eric. *William Burroughs: The Algebra of Need.* Critical Appraisal Series. London: Marion Boyars, 1977. A revised and expanded version of *William Burroughs: The Algebra of Need.* Beau Fleuve Series, no. 2, Buffalo, N.Y.: Intrepid, 1971. Mottram sees Burroughs's work as a radical critique of Western power structures and the myths that support them, classifying Burroughs as an anarchic individualist. Mottram's analysis of this theme in Burroughs's fiction and his frequent comparisons with other radical thinkers is valuable, but his unconventional style sometimes interferes with clarity.

3. Books partially devoted to Burroughs

I include here all critical books that devote a substantial discussion to Burroughs (usually a chapter) as well as the biographies and autobiographies that contain important biographical information about Burroughs.

Bowles, Paul. *Without Stopping.* New York: Putnam's, 1972. Bowles's autobiography contains valuable, although limited, information about Burroughs in Tangier and the Moroccan environment. Of particular interest is Burroughs's meeting with Gysin, drug experiments with Timothy Leary, and Burroughs's work habits in the 1960s.

Bryant, Jerry H. *The Open Decision: The Contemporary American Novel and Its Intellectual Background.* New York: Free Press, 1970, pp. 202–8. Burroughs is classified as a "hip" novelist, a satirist who plays the role of Cain, the infuriated rebel, attacking a repressive society. The metaphor of addiction is explicated in a discussion of NL, SM, and NE.

Burroughs, William, Jr. *Kentucky Ham.* New York: Dutton, 1973. Autobiography by Burroughs's son contains valuable biographical material on Burroughs and his parents, including visit of Burroughs, Jr., to Tangier and a portrait of Mortimer and Laura Burroughs.

Charters, Ann. *Kerouac: A Biography.* San Francisco: Straight Arrow, 1973. Reprint with revisions: New York: Warner Paperback Library, 1974. Biography of Kerouac includes valuable biographical information about Burroughs's friendship with Kerouac and Ginsberg and his early writings, as well as Burroughs's influence on Kerouac and his appearances in Kerouac's novels. Especially detailed on Burroughs's life from 1944 to 1953. Of the three Kerouac biographies, Charters's contains the most detail about Burroughs and his works.

Cook, Bruce. *The Beat Generation.* New York: Scribner's, 1971, pp. 165–84. A survey of the Beats, emphasizing their social, rather than literary, impact. Chapter on Burroughs discusses the fiction, primarily NL, as self-revelation and the raw data of reality; gives a brief biographical summary (several errors); and narrates an interview with Burroughs in London. The interview portion is a good portrait of Burroughs at the time.

Gifford, Barry, and Lee, Lawrence. *Jack's Book: An Oral Biography of Jack Kerouac.* New York: St. Martin's, 1978. Includes valuable biographical material by and about Burroughs, mainly up to 1953.

Ginsberg, Allen, and Cassady, Neal. *As Ever: The Collected Correspondence of Allen Ginsberg and Neal Cassady.* Berkeley: Creative Arts, 1977. The letters from 1947 to 1961 contain frequent references to Burroughs's personal life, especially his relationship with Ginsberg, and to his methods of composition.

Hendin, Josephine. *Vulnerable People, A View of American Fiction Since 1945.* New York: Oxford University Press, 1978, pp. 54–59. Discusses Burroughs as part of a group of authors whose style is called sadomasochistic. Interprets NL, SM, TTE, NE, and WB as expressions of orgiastic hatred. WB is said to be Burroughs's most violent and thus his most honest book, the culmination of the author's rage.

Kazin, Alfred. *Bright Book of Life, American Novelists and Storytellers from Hemingway to Mailer.* Boston: Little, Brown, 1973, pp. 262–70. Burroughs is classified with several other authors as an absurdist. Praised as a serious, stimulating, but obssessive writer whose only purpose is self-expression. States that Burroughs has created his own form by transcribing sexual fantasy into literary energy.

Lodge, David. *Modes of Modern Writing: Metaphor, Metonymy, and the Typology of Modern Literature.* Ithaca: Cornell University Press, 1977, pp. 35–38, 104–5, 154, 135, 252–53. A passage from NL is used as a major example in a structuralist analysis of realism, modernism, and post-modernism in fiction. As in his earlier book, Lodge finds *Naked Lunch* to be ethically and artistically confused.

———. *The Novelist at the Crossroads and Other Essays in Fiction and Criticism.* Ithaca: Cornell University Press, 1971, pp. 161–71. Sums up not only Lodge's "objections to Burroughs," but those of most other critics who prefer the tradition of the realistic novel. States that Burroughs fails as a moralist because he is deeply confused and nihilistic, and as an innovator because he is repetitious and lazy. Discusses NL and NE.

McCarthy, Mary. *The Writing on the Wall and Other Essays.* New York: Harcourt, 1970, pp. 42–53. Essay written in defense of her praise of NL at the International Writers' Conference in 1962 and probably the best single piece on Burroughs. The form of NL is compared to a movie, a ventriloquist's act, and a circus. Burroughs's repetition and obscenity are defended as part of his satire, and his "American" style of humor is defined.

McNally, Dennis. *Desolate Angel: Jack Kerouac, the Beat Generation, and America.* New York: McGraw-Hill, 1979. Biography of Kerouac contains biographical material about Burroughs that is not new, but which is clearly summarized. Good on the cultural impact of NL and Burroughs's subsequent public image.

Nelson, Cary. *The Incarnate Word: Literature and Verbal Space.* Urbana: University of Illinois Press, 1973, pp. 208–29. A reader-response approach to several literary texts, incuding a chapter on Burroughs's J, NL, SM, TTE, NE, and several shorter works. Points out that Burroughs's nonlinear prose challenges the reading process, forcing us to revise our concepts of reality. Explicates the Nova myth as an analysis of linguistic control.

Pearce, Richard. *Stages of the Clown: Perspectives on Modern Fiction from Dostoevsky to Beckett.* Carbondale: Southern Illinois University Press, 1970, pp. 88–94. NL is discussed as part of a study of the modern novel from the perspective of the ancient clown tradition. The novel is seen as "the world upside down," the apocalyptic, but vital, destruction of the world by a demonic narrator who reduces the world to chaos, but who survives through improvisation. Pearce charges Burroughs with dull, flat repetition that weakens the destructive energy of the book, making NL a minor work.

Saroyan, Aram. *Genesis Angels: The Saga of Lew Welch and the Beat Generation.* New York: Morrow, 1979. Welch's biography is juxtaposed with the popular legend of the Beats. Although Burroughs never met Welch, the sensational aspects of the Burroughs legend are employed as context for the poet's life. A good example of the persistence of Beat legend, but not factually accurate.

Seltzer, Alvin. *Chaos in the Novel: The Novel in Chaos.* New York: Schocken, 1974, pp. 330–74. Discusses Burroughs's use of random techniques, especially cutups, as a way of extending the novel form to include a vision of life as chaos and to shock us into political awareness. Comparisons with Robbe-Grillet and Genet. Prefers NL to the trilogy, which is said to be too private, repetitious, chaotic, and wholly destructive.

Tanner, Tony. *City of Words, American Fiction 1950–1970.* New York: Harper & Row, 1971, pp. 109–40. An influential survey of the contemporary American novel that devotes a lengthy chapter to Burroughs's J, YL, NL, TE, TTE, NE, and the *Paris Review* interview, also including an appendix comparing McLuhan and Burroughs. Burroughs is given major emphasis as a writer who explores the central theme of American fiction: the conflict between the dream of freedom and the dread of control. Extended comparison with John Cage.

Tytell, John. *Naked Angels: The Lives and Literature of the Beat Generation.* New York: McGraw-Hill, 1976, pp. 36–51, 111–39. The only literary history of the Beat movement, with two chapters devoted to Burroughs. Tytell places Burroughs in the tradition of decadence, symbolism, and modernism. The biographical chapter, taking Burroughs's life up to 1959, contains some errors. The critical chapter discusses seven novels (J, NL, SM, TTE, NE, WB, E), focusing on experimental technique, the "morbid beauty" of the imagery, and the theme of freedom from control.

Vernon, John. *The Garden and the Map: Schizophrenia in Twentieth Century Literature and Culture.* Urbana: University of Illinois Press, 1973, pp. 85–109. A phenomenological approach to contemporary American authors who challenge traditional Western concepts of reality and fantasy. Vernon sees Burroughs's books as maps of hell that expose and attack the "schizophrenic" structures of reality. Perceptive discussion of NL, SM, TTE, and NE, although Vernon does not always distinguish between what the author portrays and the man himself.

Werner, Craig Hansen. *Paradoxical Resolutions: American Fiction since James Joyce.* Urbana: University of Illinois Press, 1982, pp. 96–119. Analysis of TTE as an extension of some of the techniques of *Finnegans Wake* in order to disrupt the control of sociolinguistic systems.

Young, Allen. *Gay Sunshine Interview, Allen Ginsberg with Allen Young.* Bolinas, Calif.: Grey Fox, 1974. Interview with Ginsberg includes several perceptive comments on Burroughs's theory of sexuality.

4. Critical and biographical essays

This list of essays about Burroughs does not include important essays by Burroughs, Jr., Goodman, Hendin, Lodge, McCarthy, T. Tanner, and Vernon, which these authors subsequently incorporated into the books listed above. All other critical and biographical essays containing a substantial discussion of Burroughs are included. Reviews are not included.

Ansen, Alan. "Anyone Who Can Pick Up a Frying Pan Owns Death." *Big Table,* no. 2 (Summer 1959):32–41. Reprinted in *A Casebook on the Beat.* Edited by Thomas Parkinson. New York: Crowell, 1961, pp. 107–13. An important early essay by a friend and collaborator. Explains the sequence of Burroughs's early work through NL and provides biographical background, especially a portrait of Burroughs in Tangier.

Bliss, Michael. "The Orchestration of Chaos: Verbal Technique in William Burroughs' *Naked Lunch.*" *enclitic* 1 (1977):59–69. Explicates the style and organization of the many voices of NL as the basis for Burroughs's analysis of control through language. Shows that Burroughs's controversial narrative technique is controlled and thematically justified.

Bowles, Paul. "Burroughs in Tangier." *Big Table,* no. 2 (Summer 1959):42–43. Reprinted in *A Casebook on the Beat.* Edited by Thomas Parkinson. New York: Crowell, 1961, pp. 114–15. A brief but valuable portrait of Burroughs in Tangier.

Cordess, Gérard. "The Science-fiction of William Burroughs." *Caliban* 12 (1975):33–43. Discusses NL, SM, TTE, NE, and WB as avant-garde fiction that uses science-fiction motifs as metaphors for Burroughs's vision of reality, a technique that effectively challenges the reader's preconceptions. Notes significant differences between works based on the Nova conspiracy and WB.

Dorn, Edward. "Notes More or Less Relevant to Burroughs and Trocchi." *Kulchur,* no. 7 (Autumn 1962):3–22. A series of meditative notes responding to a reading of *Cain's Book* and NL, both books about addiction. Praises Burroughs's insights into social control, but criticizes the form as incoherent, the allegory as defective, thus rejecting the antiliterary technique of NL.

Gysin, Brion. "Cut-ups: A Project for Disastrous Success." *Evergreen Review,* April–May 1964, pp. 56–61. Reprinted in *The Third Mind.* Burroughs and Gysin. New York: Viking, 1978, pp. 42–51. A memoir of Burroughs and Gysin in Tangier and in Paris at the Beat Hotel. Gysin describes his discovery of the cutup technique and his first cutup experiments with Burroughs. Valuable biographical information by an important collaborator.

Hassan, Ihab. "The Literature of Silence: From Henry Miller to Beckett and Burroughs." *Encounter* 28 (January 1967):74–82. Defines "anti-literature" or "the literature of silence" as the contemporary form of the avant-garde novel. Miller, Beckett, and Burroughs are cited as the three chief examples.

———. "The Novel of Outrage, a Minority Voice in Postwar American Fiction." *American Scholar* 34 (Spring 1965):239–53. An existential interpretation of Burroughs as one of a group of authors whose works use outrage as a metaphor for the human condition. Burroughs, in NL, SM, and TTE, opposes authority with obscenity and silence.

———. "The Subtracting Machine: The Work of William S. Burroughs." *Critique* 6 (Spring 1963):4–23. Places Burroughs in the line of modern literature from Rimbaud to Beckett—the "literature of outrage," an existential category. Discusses J, TE, NL, SM, and TTE. For Burroughs, reality is a "death machine" made up of words, and cutups are a "subtracting machine" that can destroy the Logos of creation. Burroughs is criticized because he affirms nothing and gives no place to love in his works.

Hilfer, Anthony Channell. "Mariner and Wedding Guest in William Burroughs' 'Naked Lunch.'" *Criticism* 22 (1980):252–65. A detailed analysis of the narrative voice in NL. The thesis is that the action of the novel is "the moment by moment relation of narrator and reader," the only two characters in the book. The narrator is an ambivalent participant in and satirist of his own narrative comparable to Coleridge's Ancient Mariner. Hilfer's analysis justifies the ambivalent nature of the narrator, which many critics have seen as a flaw.

Kostelanetz, Richard. "From Nightmare to Serendipity: A Retrospective Look at William Burroughs." *Twentieth Century Literature* 11 (October 1965):123–30. Calls NL a modern classic, part of the new drug literature, which portrays contemporary existence as a horrifying world of total sickness. Connects Burroughs with several other modern writers who see the modern city as hell.

Lee, Robert A. "William Burroughs and the Sexuality of Power." *20th Century Studies,* no. 2 (November 1969):74–88. An analysis of imagery and structure in J, NL, SM, TTE, and NE, stressing Burroughs's theme of the sexuality of power as the basis for a mythology. Praises Burroughs as a serious moralist and social critic.

Lydenberg, Robin. "Cut-Up: Negative Poetics in William Burroughs and Roland Barthes." *Comparative Literature Studies* 15 (December 1978):414–30. Discusses the relationship between Burroughs's fiction and structuralism, comparing Burroughs's cutup technique to Barthes's *découpage*. Sees the two authors as similar in their attacks upon traditional linguistic and literary controls.

Manganotti, Donatella. "The Final Fix." *Kulchur* 4 (Autumn 1964):76–87. The only critical essay devoted to YL, which Manganotti discusses in relation to Burroughs's other works. Taking the book as a whole, she analyzes the development of Burroughs's persona, imagery, and themes. Discusses the drug yage as central to Burroughs's vision.

McConnell, Frank D. "William Burroughs and the Literature of Addiction." *Massachusetts Review* 8 (1967):665–80. Discusses NL as part of the English-American romantic literature of addiction, with an extended comparison to Coleridge. Analyzes addiction as the basis for a powerful literary vision that is antisymbolic and antiliterary.

McLuhan, Marshall. "Notes on Burroughs." *Nation,* 28 December 1964, pp. 517–19. Interprets NL and NE as illustrations of McLuhan's theories about how the technological environment influences consciousness. Calls Burroughs a prophet who describes the new electric environment and warns against its dangers, in a discontinuous style that reflects his subject matter.

Mertz, Robert. "The Virus Visions of William Burroughs." *Itinerary 3: Criticism.* Edited by Frank Baldanza. Bowling Green, Ohio: Bowling Green University Press, 1977, pp. 11–18. Discusses NL, SM, TTE, and NE as a critique of the mass media. The thesis that Burroughs is allied with conservative critics of popular culture is debatable.

Michelson, Peter. "Beardsley, Burroughs, Decadence, and the Poetics of Obscenity." *Tri-Quarterly,* no. 12 (Spring 1968):139–55. Places NL in the literary tradition of decadence. Burroughs's art is truthful rather than beautiful, and his truth is ugly because he reveals a demonic world of technocrats who define man as consumer.

Oxenhandler, Neal. "Listening to Burroughs' Voice." *Surfiction: Fiction Now . . . and Tomorrow.* Edited by Raymond Federman. Chicago: Swallow, 1975, pp. 181–201. A "psychocritique" of the infantile fantasies of violence and perversion, which are "the substance of Burroughs' novels." Discusses J, NL, SM, TTE, and NE. This Freudian analysis of sadomasochistic image patterns sheds light on the psychic ambivalence that many critics have deplored, although the analysis is sometimes reductive. Burroughs's work affirmed as part of a major tradition that includes Kafka and Beckett.

Palumbo, Donald. "William Burroughs' Quartet of Science Fiction Novels as Dystopian Social Satire." *Extrapolation* 20 (1979):321–29. NL, SM, TTE, and NE are not pure science fiction, but novels of ideas that use the trappings of science fiction. A good summary of the Nova mythology as the science-fiction fantasy that provides the single plot for the four novels.

Peterson, R. G. "A Picture Is a Fact: Wittgenstein and *The Naked Lunch*." *Twentieth Century Literature* 12 (July 1966):78–86. Reprinted in *The Beats: Essays in Criticism*. Edited by Lee Bartlett. Jefferson, N.C.: McFarland, 1981, pp. 30–39. NL interpreted as a literary representation of Wittgenstein's *Tractatus Logico-Philosophicus*, which Peterson says defines a terrifying solipsistic world of meaningless, disconnected facts and an unknowable self. Peterson's interpretation of Wittgenstein is debatable. He finds both the *Tractatus* and NL terrifying because they attack traditional concepts of self and reality.

Russell, Charles. "Individual Voice in the Collective Discourse: Literary Innovation in Postmodern American Fiction." *Sub-stance: A Review of Theory and Literary Criticism*, no. 27 (1980):29–39. Defines, in poststructuralist terms, the postmodernist aesthetic of several contemporary American writers, often using Burroughs as the touchstone.

Skau, Michael. "The Central Verbal System: The Prose of William Burroughs." *Style* 15 (1981):401–14. An analysis of the stylistic strategies Burroughs uses to combat verbal manipulation and the resulting paradox of self-destructive linguistic experiments. Examples are drawn from Burroughs's entire body of work to 1980.

Skerl, Jennie. "A Beat Chronology: 1944–64." *Moody Street Irregulars, A Jack Kerouac Newsletter*, nos. 5/6 (Winter/Spring 1980):11–14. Revised and enlarged: "A Beat Chronology, the First Twenty-Five Years: 1944–1969." *Dictionary of Literary Biography*, vol. 16. *The Beats: Literary Bohemians in Postwar America*. Edited by Ann Charters. Detroit: Gale Research, 1983, pp. 593–606. A chronology of the Beat movement, focusing primarily on Burroughs, Ginsberg, and Kerouac, and including eight other authors. Provides a detailed chronology of Burroughs's life and work and his interrelationships with other Beat writers.

————. "William S. Burroughs: Pop Artist." *Sphinx*, no. 11 (1980):1–15. The only essay to analyze in detail the content and purpose of Burroughs's use of popular culture in his work and the significance of the "carny world" as the source of Burroughs's vision. Defines Burroughs as a pop artist. Discusses J, NL, SM, TTE, and NE.

Stull, William L. "The Quest and the Question: Cosmology and Myth in the Work of William S. Burroughs, 1953–60." *Twentieth Century Literature* 24 (Summer 1978):225–42. Reprinted in *The Beats: Essays in Criticism*. Edited by Lee Bartlett. Jefferson, N.C.: McFarland, 1981, pp. 14–29. Counters the usual critical emphasis on Burroughs's novelty with the thesis that the familiar quest pattern structures all of his fiction from J to NE, although Stull discusses only J, "In Search of Yage," and NL. A good analysis of the quest in Burroughs's fiction, stressing parallels with the grail legend.

Tanner, James E., Jr. "Experimental Styles Compared: E. E. Cummings and William Burroughs." *Style* 10 (1976):1–27. A comparison of graphic and linguistic transformations in the poetry of Cummings and in NL, showing similar techniques and effects in authors holding opposing philosophies. Burroughs is said to be a less radical experimentalist than Cummings, but flaws in the design of this comparative study call this finding into question.

Tytell, John. "Conversation with Allen Ginsberg." *Partisan Review* 41 (1974):253–62. A great deal of the interview focuses on Ginsberg's friendship with Burroughs and Kerouac, Burroughs's intellectual influence upon Ginsberg, and Ginsberg's explication of Burroughs's theories of art, language, and social control and deconditioning.

Weinstein, Arnold. "Freedom and Control in the Erotic Novel: The Classical *Liaisons dangereuses* Versus the Surrealist *Naked Lunch.*" *Dada/Surrealism*, no. 10/11 (1982):29–38. Compares the two novels on the basis of the same theme (body control and human connection) and the same plot (the desire to possess another), showing that each work is a *cas-limite* of classical (*Liaisons*) versus surrealist (NL) form. Also shows how the works illuminate each other and the concept of the body in Western culture.

Index

Weissner, Carl, 16
Wild Boys, The, 5, 16, 75, 76, 81–84; as
    film montage, 81; themes of, 82;
    wild boys, fantasy of, 79, 83–84
Williams, Tennessee, 14
"Word-and-image" technique, 3

Yage Letters, The (collaboration with
    Ginsberg), 10, 20, 31–33; expansion
    of drug persona, 32; homosexuality,
    importance of, 31; quest of
    protagonist, 31–32; "routine,"
    introduction of, 32